Don't Tell Me What To Do... Ask Me

Creating Egalitarian Relationships from a Gestalt Perspective

by

Cyndy Sheldon, MSW

Bellingham, Washington

2016

Don't Tell Me What To Do... Ask Me!
Creating Egalitarian Relationships from a Gestalt Perspective
by Cyndy Sheldon

First Edition
Copyright ©2016 Cyndy Sheldon
ISBN-13: 978-1533697295

http://www.cyndysheldon.com

Cover illustration by Angela Anderson
Other illustrations by Paula Forget
Book design and typography: Kathleen Weisel, weiselcreative.com

Dedicated

to

Fritz and Laura Perls

Virginia Satir

and to my parents

Sally and Jack Sheldon

Contents

PREFACE

Although this book is about couples and partnerships, it also includes a lot of references to Gestalt principles and practices, as these are oriented towards relating in a healthy way. My book *Gestalt As a Way of Life: Awareness Practices,* might be useful to the reader as an adjunct to this one. Both books are available through my website: CyndySheldon.com, or at Amazon.com in the US, UK and EU.

I've written this book in a simple format in order to help the reader easily find a section he or she wants to read about. Most of the chapters are short and to the point. Experiments are offered for individuals and couples to try, to see if they are useful in exploring personal awareness as well as awareness in your relationships.

- Key are the sections on Structuring an Egalitarian Relationship, Healthy Relationships, and Unhealthy Dynamics.

- You can read the book from beginning to end, or go to the Table of Contents and pick a chapter that interests you.

- Or you can just close your eyes and let your hands find a page, and see what this oracle has for you today...

- If you are a therapist, put these books in your waiting room... a client's quick perusal can lead them to a lot of good work with you during the session!

Section A

Introduction

1. What is an Egalitarian Relationship?

2. Purpose and Goals of This Book

3. My Personal Story

EGALITARIAN RELATIONSHIP

Two people who claim they are a couple, or partners, or lovers, who decide together the way they want to organize and live their lives. This does not necessarily mean they have to do everything 50-50. They just have to agree. There may be some items that are non-negotiable, which both can say they insist on. And with these items, it is up to the other to agree or not.

EGALITARIAN

(from French *égalitaire*, from *égalité*, equality, from Latin *aequālitās*, *aequālis*, equal)

> This word is an adjective, meaning: affirming, promoting, or characterized by a belief in equal political, economic, social, and civil rights for all people.

It does not include the personal, but I use it in this new way about relationships, as I think it fits perfectly.

RELATIONSHIP

(re·la·tion·ship (rĭ-lā′shən-shĭp′)

> This word is a noun meaning: The condition or fact of being related; connection or association. Connection by blood or marriage; kinship. A particular type of connection existing between people related to or having dealings with each other: has a close relationship with his siblings. A romantic or sexual involvement.

1. What is an Egalitarian Relationship?

This concept came to me in meditation a few years ago.. It is such a fitting definition of what I am writing about, so I decided to use it. Most people I talk to seem to understand it once they think about it. And many say "what does egalitarian mean?" The word comes from *egalitaire,* a French word meaning *equal.* An egalitarian relationship is about two equal people, who call themselves a couple or partners. They probably, although not necessarily, live together, sleep together, and say they have an intimate primary relationship.

> *They make their decisions jointly, which could mean they decide together that one of them is the boss of the kitchen, or the boss of the electronic equipment.*

SMALL BUSINESS

Most partners, living in the same place, are running a small business together (their household) which may include paying the bills, paying taxes, managing a house or apartment and spending a lot of time together. To see it as a relationship business helps many to be more responsible to each other, and to make sure all things are in order. They create a *structure* together that they can both live with. They are *explicit*, not implicit, as to what the structure includes. They don't have to agree that half has to be done or earned by each. One person might make twice as much money as the other and they might decide to pay proportionately for the bills. Or they might find some other creative way to divide things. If one can't pay half of what they owe each month, another way would be to do other work for their relationship business, perhaps doing physical work in the yard, or selling one's artwork to contribute to the pot.

There are no *shoulds* about what they agree to: they could decide *together* to do things the way their grandparents did, where the roles were clear cut: one is the breadwinner, the other the homemaker. And if one of their agreements doesn't work, they can decide together to change things.

It is my sense that more and more modern USA relationships are egalitarian or almost egalitarian. Many couples will say *yes* when asked if they have this type of relationship. But usually they haven't been very explicit or clear, and they haven't considered many aspects of their lives together. This lack of clarity in those areas that are *not* explicit leaves a vacuum for:

- unclear expectations
- conflict
- misunderstandings
- pain, hurt and anger

The couple below thought they had an egalitarian relationship, but in fact it was only true regarding their finances. They hadn't talked about any other equal aspects of their household structure. So when things started going badly for them, they fell back to those relationship ways of behaving they had learned from their parents.

Judy and Ted had been together for two years, dividing their finances up 50-50, as they made about the same amount. Suddenly they were faced with a huge dilemma.

Ted lost his job. Now Judy was the only one bringing in any money. They had not prepared for such an eventuality, even though they knew the country was facing a loss of jobs which were going overseas. They had no contingency plan for such a problem.

Frightened, they both became anxious and ended up blaming each other. She forgot they decided their relationship would be egalitarian, and fell back into the old paradigm where she expected he'd be the breadwinner, not her. So her expectations of him to find a job were unreasonable given his training. And they were unexpected.

She became scared and angry. He fell back into the old paradigm as well, and began blaming himself for not taking care of his wife as head of the household, he also blamed her for not supporting him psychologically as well as financially.

They both reverted back to a more hierarchical way of being with one another when this crisis occurred. They were used to this, as most of their lives had been spent in such authoritarian settings.

They had both been children beholden to their parents; they had both been students under the watchful eyes of their teachers; and they had both been employees under the thumbs of their employers. Only with a couple of friends did they have a vague semblance of an equal relationship, and these didn't involve any of the baggage that goes with living together, pooling their resources, and making decisions.

You can see how little experience most of us have had in egalitarian relationships. It is quite amazing, especially since we supposedly live in a democratic society.

"I'm used to being given orders and if I don't obey, there are consequences. I had never thought about things being different than this until recently."

EXPERIMENTS
for you and your partner to do to enhance your awareness of yourself and your partner.

1. *Make a list of all the hierarchies you have been in, both at the top of the ladder and at the bottom.*
2. *Describe to one another what you liked and didn't like about each of them.*
3. *Discuss what egalitarian organizations and relationships you have been in, if any.*
4. *Describe how they were for you: did you like them, why or why not.*
5. *Observe where your discussion takes you as you explore this theme .*

2.   Purpose and Goals of This Book

This book is for those who want an Egalitarian Relationship
rather than a Hierarchical, or Authoritarian one,
regardless of how benevolent it might be.

In my experience a large percentage of those of us who seek help from therapists are mostly concerned about our primary relationships. This includes help in understanding the roles we are playing in our dysfunctional relating, and suggestions for healthier options to experiment with at the end of each chapter.

1. This book is for all *couples* who are struggling to make their relationships work better.

2. Basically I've created the *overarching concept, Egalitarian Relationships*, to help us organize our understanding of our relationships from a broader perspective than we might be using currently to understand one another. What we as therapists and counselors have been teaching our clients is more than love and respect; we've been teaching them to treat one another equally and uniquely.

3. I address in detail ways we can *co-create an agreed upon structure* which is very explicit. Over the past few years the participants in my egalitarian relationship classes have added to the list of topics they felt needed to be addressed.

4. Being *explicit* can lessen our misunderstanding and conflict, as then expectations are clear to each of us. This counteracts the vague and unclear ideas many of us bring to a relationship from our previous experiences, including the expectations we grew up with. For example:

   One couple, Alice and Barry, made clear decisions about their finances, vacations, and other big issues, but they never agreed about what chores each was responsible for. So Barry ended up asking Alice every now and then, "What can I do to help?" At first she loved that he offered to help her! But after some time, she realized he was assuming that she was in charge of the household (as was his mother and grandmother). He thought he was being a good egalitarian by asking how he could help. After awhile she began to resent being put in the role of household manager, which she hadn't agreed to. Many conflicts later, she finally saw the obvious, which had been out of her awareness. Finally they talked about it, and reorganized some of their tasks to make them more **explicit***, which was a relief to them both.*

5. The relationship structure can be *fluid and flexible* to allow for change as our lives progress as we go from one stage to another. What worked for us as young adults might change over time.

6. To *raise our awareness* about authoritarian and egalitarian relationships and organizations. Awareness can lead to more choice as uncomfortable as it may be at times.

   Many men still unconsciously believe they "must be the head of the household and protect their women and children." Many women take for granted they are in charge of the home including child rearing, and must go along with their mates.

   Lesbian and Gay couples may have a heads up on Heterosexual couples because the old paradigm above doesn't cover same sex marriages. So they may not have a lot of historical training to undo, unless they specifically identify with being a male or female in their same sex marriages. They, like everyone else, still have to deal with the dysfunctional roles and games they may have played since childhood.

7. To encourage all twosomes to *develop their abilities* to work together, to negotiate, to compromise, and to create a win-win for both. These skills would model for their

children and others how to be in the world they are inheriting.

Currently, too many children see their parents not working well together, bickering and fighting, unable to negotiate and compromise, so they are left full of grief, hurt, and resentment. No one wins. Or they see their single parent often in the role of having to take care of everything. This naturally means that there is no time to be with each other. More grief, hurt and resentment can follow.

8. Also this book is for those of us *psychotherapists and counselors*, to give us more ways to look at partnering, which hopefully will help our clients understand and improve their relationships with one another.

9. And lastly, this book is to help all couples make more room in their lives together to "follow their bliss," a saying by well-known Joseph Campbell, scholar, writer and teacher. To feel alive and vibrant we all need to know what helps us feel that way, and then we can create the time and space to have these opportunities. We need to find ways to refuel our souls!

3.   **My Personal Story**

While I was in graduate school in Berkeley California in 1962, I attended a Dream Seminar in Gestalt Therapy led by Fritz Perls, and soon after that a Virginia Satir lecture-demonstration on family therapy. I was more than inspired, in fact I knew then that their teachings were going to be the foundation of the work I'd be doing for the rest of my life. I'm now 80 and still teaching Gestalt and Couples therapy, as well as writing about it.

I made sure I found my way to their programs. In 1967, at the request of Fritz Perls MD, co-founder of Gestalt Therapy, I started the (original) Gestalt Institute of San Francisco with three colleagues. In 1968 I was invited to work at The Family Therapy Institute of Marin, a Virginia Satir-oriented training center, which wanted a Gestalt therapist and teacher on their staff. Later I taught family and couples therapy with colleagues at the Melange Institute in the Bay Area as well. For 25 years I taught Gestalt, not only in San Francisco, but in Europe as well.

Then in 1991 I moved to Northern Arizona where I immersed myself in two new worlds: the world of spirituality of many flavors in the New Age Mecca of Sedona; and the Navajo Reservation, where I worked part time with the elders, medicine people and others at a very *avant garde* Indian Health Service clinic in Winslow, AZ. Here I discovered similarities between Gestalt and Navajo ways of life, ran wellness conferences Indian-style, taught classes all over the Reservation called Healing the Workplace, and ran the Medicine Man program, the first of its kind in the country. I continued seeing individuals and couples in my private practice in Sedona and Flagstaff. I co-led week-long workshops on Gestalt Therapy and the Navajo Way of Life, and in the process discovered some similarities between the two approaches to life. The Navajo people know how to be present with one another, just as we teach trainees in Gestalt therapy. Taking time to be with one another, and leaving the many hierarchies of our lives behind, we met egalitarian style. This is just one of the similarities!

After 15 fascinating years in Arizona I packed my bags and moved to Bellingham, Washington, guided by unseen forces which know me better than I know myself. When I got here, some of my relatives moved nearby, and I discovered many I didn't know existed on the other side of the mountains! By then it was 2006 and I was 70 years old, so I got to work spearheading some Gestalt trainings in Seattle and Bellingham, wrote my first book *Gestalt as a Way of Life*, and expanded the concept of Egalitarian Relationships, which has led to many workshops about this theme, as well as this book.

Along the way I was deeply influenced by the Human Potential Movement of the 1960s, as well as everything else that was going on in the Bay Area at that time, including the Women's Movement. Gestalt colleagues and I started an inexpensive drop-in group for women, called *Alyssum*, which gave many women the support they needed as they realized they were equal to men, and who then had to face all the repercussions of expanding their understanding of themselves and their worlds.

Equality in those days was really more about jobs, equal pay, and less about the intricacies of relationships. We did deal with such at the Family Therapy Institute, but not to the extent that is happening now in 2016, as again cries explode all over the world for equality in our governments, organizations and relationships. The hierarchies of religions, governments, and corporations are falling apart, more so than ever in my lifetime.

Many people are waking up to the fact that they have lived in hierarchies most of their lives whether at jobs, religious institutions, organizations, and in partnerships and marriages. As I review my life, I realize I have had more opportunities than most to be in co-operative or egalitarian organizations, and haven't suffered the consequences of hierarchies as much as many have, except the winds of the times were definitely not very egalitarian!

Some examples of my unusual experiences were:

- As a young person I was part of a Quaker Meeting (church), which was an organization run by *consensus*. Also there, I participated in my first act of rebellion when the entire Sunday School quit in protest of one of the policies adopted by the elders.

I was 13 at this time and felt empowered as we all marched out because the elders couldn't come to consensus about contributing a donation to a nearby Synagogue that was being built.

- I was well schooled in Civics, and recall being very active in high school in student government. We took a lot of pride in following democratic principles.
- Even though my parents had a benign authoritarian relationship, meaning my father did everything he could as head of the family, to *let* my mother do what she wanted. (However, as a good dutiful wife she rarely asked for anything!)
- I, along with about 15 other college kids, participated in an American Friends Service Committee (Quaker Social Service group) work camp in a Mexican village for two months. We learned to honor the villagers and not impose our ideas on them, but to work together in an egalitarian manner on a few projects for the village.
- When I finished college in 1957 I got a job traveling for World University Service (WUS), a social service arm of the National Students Association at that time. This NSA was an egalitarian organization, *I thought,* run by elected students from all over the USA. I felt honored and proud to be representing them through WUS, giving speeches and guiding colleges to raise money for our projects which funded student health centers in third world countries, students who had to flee areas of war and conflict for a new life in the USA, and other programs. I discovered a few years later that NSA & WUS were not egalitarian at all, but were secretly funded and run by the CIA! What a shock this was to my 25-year-old self! In 2015, a book came out titled, *Patriotic Betrayal* by Karen Paget and published by Yale U Press, about the details of those times. What a shock.
- My marriage in the early 1960s was to a man who had a lot of experience learning about himself and others as a student of psychology and sociology. He believed in equality for all, and as a result our marriage was more egalitarian than most at that time, although definitely not totally! But then none of us knew much better at that time anyway!

- When colleagues and I started the original Gestalt Institute of San Francisco in 1967, we created it as a co-operative, where all 10 staff members made the decisions. We learned how hard this is to do, and yet rewarding. I also worked at the Family Therapy Institute at the same time, which had an authoritarian, although benevolent, structure. Its authoritarian structure fell apart, while the structure of the Gestalt Institute kept on going. It was a profound learning experience for me in those years to compare the two organizations' way of being structured and their effects on the staff members of each organization. The Gestalt staff were much more empowered, whereas the staff at the Family Therapy Institute were much more subservient.
- In my 70s I got involved with the co-housing movement, with the hope that we'd begin such a co-operative senior community where I now live. Unfortunately, the project fell through, but I gained a lot of experience by struggling with trying to make it happen.

As for the many hierarchical organizations I was part of, here is a brief list:
- My family of origin.
- All of the schools I attended including college and university.
- My jobs at the Navy Hospital, the Indian Health Service, the Family Therapy Institute, World University Service (CIA funded), Senior Connections which places therapists in nursing homes, and an alternative health clinic in Sedona.

As we are facing elections in the USA in 2016 two front runners, one from each party, are busy challenging the lack of democratic principles being followed in both parties. The theme is the same as that in relationships. People want to be treated as equals and they want to be understood.

※

Section B

Background

1. Historical and Sociological Perspective

2. Brief History of Relationships in the USA

3. Human Potential Movement, 1960s

4. Egalitarian Roots in Gestalt Therapy

5. The Women's Movement of the 1970s
   and Its Effects on Relationships

6. LGBT Movement

7. When People First Meet

8. The Many Hierarchies in Our Lives

9. Global Impasse: Transition Time

1. Historical and Sociological Perspective

"Columbus and his successors were not coming to an empty wilderness, but into a world, which in some places was as densely populated as Europe, and where the culture was complex, where human relations were more egalitarian *than in Europe, and where the relations between men, women, children and nature were more beautifully worked out than perhaps any other places in the world."*

– Howard Zinn, quote from his book titled *The People's History of the United States.*

THE BIG PICTURE: A TIME OF TRANSITION

Over the past 75 years in the USA and many other places on our planet, we've seen that millions of people have lost their jobs, their incomes, their health, and other rights; police have become militarized; corporations have stolen from the people and defied the laws, and governments have been bought off by them. National hierarchies have become global hierarchies, which have increasingly dominated all of us. In the process not only have humans been denigrated, but our beautiful planet has been as well.

A friend who lived in Hawaii for 20 years, returned to the mainland as she could not handle all of the pollution in the air, water and land created by the US military, as well as by many corporations.

Corruption and lies are commonplace. Our democratic values have all but disappeared, and schools nowadays often do not teach Civics anymore. So the younger generations have no training in how to live in a democracy, much less see the value of one.

Our Democratic Republic, our Constitution, and our Bill of Rights have lost a lot of their value. And from all reports similar problems are happening in other democratic countries in the Western world.

Yet, throughout this time period, more and more people have been crying for equality of all sorts. We've seen and heard from those of all races, cultures, religions, genders, old, young, even the animal world, crying for more humane treatment and a voice in the process.

> *"We want equality in our government, equality in our marketplace, equality in our workplace, equality in our homes, and equality in our relationships." "NO MORE AUTHORITARIANS TELLING US WHAT TO DO!" they cry over and over again.*

The authoritarians who have been in charge, often surreptitiously, have ignored the people for too long now.

More and more people are waking up and seeing that they've been subjugated without fully realizing it. As many have asked, "Where is the outrage?" I think that outrage is happening now. People from both ends of the political spectrum in the USA are rebelling and refusing to go along with those in power.

The Diagnostic and Statistical Manual of Mental Disorders (DSM IV & V) now tells us that *rebelling* might be a psychiatric disorder. To me, though peoples' behavior may be self defeating, it can be a sign of health, a sign that a person's soul is alive and well inside them… that we are all equal, and we are going to continue to demand and fight for equality.

This rebelliousness has been like a wave, with some corners of the globe creating more egalitarian communities, while another area of the globe is creating more educational opportunities which inspires more people to choose egalitarian lives, to other areas that are encouraging individuals to treat their *inner* selves with more respect and equality, rather than criticizing their every move. And the wave goes on and on, sometimes seeming to diminish, other times exploding.

And at the same time the powers-that-be are becoming more violent. These times in the early part of the 21st Century are complicated with ups and downs, and yet the inner souls of the people seem to be slowly, in a spiral-like movement, rising to the top. We see this change happening in many aspects of our lives from the societal to families, to couples, and to each of our inner beings, as we treat ourselves with greater love and respect. The words most people use don't include the word *egalitarian*, but rather they use the words: freedom, equality, and empowered.

In terms of relationships, slowly the pendulum has been moving from an *authoritarian* model to an increased desire for an *egalitarian* model on every level of our existence.

THE HUMAN POTENTIAL MOVEMENT AND THE RISE OF FAMILY AND COUPLES THERAPY IN THE USA DURING THE 1960S AND '70S.

In the late 1960s in the San Francisco Bay Area, as the counterculture and the Human Potential Movement were in full swing, Virginia Satir's family and couples therapy teachings became very popular. Her approach—honoring each individual, working directly and openly—was a departure from some of the earlier family approaches which involved more manipulative techniques to create change in family structures. Her approach—along with the humanist approaches of Fritz Perls and Gestalt Therapy, Abraham Maslow, Carl Rogers, Eric Berne and others were also evolving then—and all of these approaches had a profound impact on individual and couples psychotherapy. Therapists were treating their clients as equals who needed help through more education and experiential teachings, rather than because they were sick and needed a doctor's help. They were part of the emerging Human Potential Movement, starting mostly at Esalen in Big Sur. Fritz and Virginia both taught there, and influenced one another during those years.

Although Virginia's style encouraged couples to be open with one another, and to treat one another as equals, no one was using the term *Egalitarian Relationships* at that time. Couples were still getting into conflict with one another's gamey ways of trying to get what they wanted from each other. They were still making lots of assumptions, based on the roles of their parents and the cultural ways of those who had emigrated here from all over the globe, without checking in with one another. People were reluctant to discuss the nitty-gritty of things for fear of scaring their new romantic partner away. So a lot was pushed under the rug, and only the compulsive ones did their homework of getting clear about what they could expect from one another.

In the meantime, most of us, without awareness, have been subjected to one hierarchy or another. Very few of us have ever been in an egalitarian relationship or organization. For example, we were all children under the thumb of parents, students beholden to teachers, and employees responsible to employers. Then we moved into one of the top hierarchical roles as we got old enough, such as parent, teacher, and boss.

A few hundred years ago, marriages were based on the husband being in charge of the family, another hierarchical structure, and the woman was the homemaker. The roles between the marriage partners were clear and defined. Most everyone knew what to expect back then.

During WWII, many women worked in factories all over the USA to make needed items for the war. Afterwards, more and more women went to colleges and had careers. Eventually families needed two incomes to survive in the increasingly expensive economy.

The women's movement sparked a lot of changes as well, but again they weren't clearly defined on the home front, particularly in heterosexual partnerships that were still burdened by the old roles. But during this time, women began to value themselves more and attended women's groups for support from other women. Those of us interviewed by Anne Kent Rush for her book in 1973, called *Getting Clear*, ran a drop-in group for women for $3 a session in San Francisco.

> *Anne Kent Rush compiled a book called* Getting Clear *about the Women's Movement which became known all over Europe as well as in the US. I found it in a book store in Edinburgh, Scotland, in the late 1970s, much to my surprise. She interviewed a number of family/couples therapists as well as Gestalt therapists, including me, for this book, which is still available today.*

So what happened was that a lot of women decided they had to do it all, and many became multitasking **superwomen**. Many were married, and many were single mothers and in the workforce. Lesbian and gay relationships seemed to have a better chance of partners being equals, as they didn't have the old societal baggage from their parents as much as heterosexual couples had. However, they still played all the same psychological games to manipulate each other, just like everyone else.

Also at this time in the 1960s and '70s more and more partnered with people of different ethnic groups, religions, and races, further complicating relationship structures. Cultural differences often caused confusion in expectations of the couple, and many also struggled with how to deal with prejudice from others towards them, or one of them, or from parents who didn't accept their partners. And many heterosexual couples broke up when one of the parties came out and chose to be with someone of the same sex.

TODAY IN 2016

As a result there was a lot of room for confusion, misunderstanding and conflict. Couples began to wonder what was going on, as more and more became single again and again.

The old well-defined roles of earlier generations, within more culturally consistent boundaries, gave way to chaos and **unexpected expectations** as people partnered across many boundaries. Children had a rough time, and still do, as their parents got to know themselves better and turned against the status quo to follow their inner guidance, in ways their partner, and perhaps the children, didn't agree to.

There are no common standards like there used to be, except perhaps within subgroups that haven't intermingled with other groups much, such as the Amish in Pennsylvania, Ohio and Iowa.

For about 10 years I worked on the Navajo Reservation, and they had very specific values that their people were not to marry outside their tribe, including someone from another nearby tribe. This had a lot to do with their secret ceremonies and ways of life. However, now this is changing too, as more and more Navajos leave the reservation to get an education or work, and there they meet people of other cultures who have different expectations for partnering.

Needless to say, there has been a lot of work for family and couples therapists over the past 50 years, as everyone has been struggling, counselors included, to make sense of the *huge transition* that is going on, not just in the USA, but in many other countries as well.

CUSTOMIZE!

Since there are no clear guidelines, each couple will have to create their own structure… by customizing it to fit the two of them. Ideally this would require they talk at length with one another about what they want, what their values are, and how they want to accomplish their goals together, so that it is a win-win structure for both. And the more **explicit** they can be, the better. It is a lot of work, and the sooner they begin to do this, the less likely unforeseen expectations will arise and cause chaos in their lives!

Men and women who don't create a structure, live in vagueness and innuendo. I hear many people interpreting their partner's behavior about different themes they have not been explicit about. They are often filled with anxiety as to whether he or she is upset with them.

> One time a client went on and on trying to mind-read her partner's feelings about her going on a retreat with a male friend. He knew about it. She was very anxious about this, and wanted me to try to analyze his vague response when she told him. I refused and suggested she ask him. She had never considered this! All their life together, some 40 years, she rarely asked him such personal questions. And she had no awareness of what she was doing to make herself anxious. In this situation, she went home and asked him, and he was fine with her plan. In fact, he was delighted she'd asked him, as it made him feel considered. And in addition, he was glad she'd be away that weekend as he had to finish an article he was writing, and he told her that he can work better when the house is quiet.

She slowly let go of her mind-reading, created a more explicit understanding with him about many of their vague ways of being together, and she became much more relaxed and happy in her marriage.

Many say they don't want to be explicit about such controversial topics as having children for fear of scaring their partner off. Perhaps the truth is exactly what is needed!

> *When Mary had a child, and they had never fully shared their feelings about doing so, she ended up being the caretaker. He offered to help now and then, but he had mixed feelings about having children, and she sensed his unhappiness and resentment, even though he tried not to show his feelings. She and her husband both work outside the home, and Mary, who is overworked and stressed out, often ends up telling him what to do. She is not very loving, and resents all that she is doing. He became resentful with her constantly telling him what to do. She realizes eventually that they had never made a clear and explicit joint decision about having children, and if they did who would do what differently.*

And as you can see he isn't able to handle her being busy all the time as well as resentful. This sounds like a lose-lose situation to me.

People who are scared by what their partners want should clarify and work things out before it is too late. Or they should leave now, so children aren't born into an insecure environment with a single parent who will surely be stressed by trying to do everything, by being a *super-parent.*

2.   Brief History of Relationships in The USA

"I want to love you without clutching, appreciate you without judging, join you without invading, invite you without demanding, leave you without guilt, criticize you without blaming, and help you without insulting. If I can have the same from you, then we can truly meet and enrich each other."

– Virginia Satir

Three and four hundred years ago, before there was such a thing as counseling or psychotherapy, families and couples in the United States found ways to deal with their differences. Many were part of religious communities where they could get help if need be from ministers, pastors and so forth, and many did what they could to resolve their differences by themselves. After the development of individual psychotherapy—following Freud and Jung's theories taking hold in the USA—children's therapists were trained. During those earlier years, there was no such thing as couples or family therapy basically until the 1960s.

Problems were seen as mental health issues and single members of families were treated by individual therapists for such. It was referred to as the "Medical Model." If someone had a problem they went to see a psychiatrist, as they were "sick."

In those early days men and women knew what their family roles were. They were pretty standardized. Women and men knew what was expected of them. So everyone could make assumptions about their partners and probably be accurate: she would be the homemaker and he would be the breadwinner. They knew what expectations they could have of one another. Life seemed simpler then. But these roles might not have been good roles for all men and women. Peoples' individual talents and skills were not always honored in this process. But these were clear expectations, and most people followed them.

Then came the world wars, and women went to work in factories and other places while their men went off to war. Then the cries for equality started, and eventually the women's movement began in the 1970s. Things began to change then for many women. Different kinds of relationships became more frequent. Roles changed. People tried to find out what they were best suited for, and this ushered in a whole new dynamic: people might be able to follow their bliss, as Joseph Campbell said, and still be in meaningful relationships.

As exciting as this was for women, a strange thing happened in those years. Very few changed their traditional roles. Instead, women decided to become *supermoms* or settled for being single moms when the couple parted or divorced. Supermom meant she did her career and all the usual household things as well: cooking, cleaning, child caretaking, etc., at least in the middle class. Men pretty much kept to the old role of provider, when he could get a job in order to provide for his family.

By this time things were becoming chaotic. Women were becoming exhausted from all the hard work, and resenting it. Many became ill and overwhelmed, leading to more and more appointments with doctors and eventually psychotherapists... and more and more pills, prescription as well as other kinds. Women, the family caretakers, took on the blame for dysfunctional relationships and sought help to fix these... and often their mates didn't participate in these counseling sessions.

When I first got out of graduate school in 1962, it seemed that in the San Francisco Bay Area at least, most psychotherapists were men. This gradually changed over the years as more and more women went into the field, and since most clients were women, they began seeking out women as their therapists.

All of this was going on before the advent of couples and family therapy, which finally emerged in the late 1950s and '60s, thanks to people like Carl Whitaker and Virginia Satir, pioneers in the field of family therapy. They put family and couples therapy on the map.

I was trained in the Satir approach to families and couples. Her work honored men and women as equals, and although she didn't have people structuring their relationships as I am attempting to teach here, she treated everyone as an equal. It was part of who she was, and her training as a social worker also emphasized this.

Luckily for those of us trained in her approach, a cry for more equality was heard everywhere, particularly in families and relationships. At the same time Fritz Perls was developing Gestalt Therapy at Esalen Institute in Big Sur, where he met Virginia. They respected one another, and influenced one another. Both honored the uniqueness of everyone, and the creativity of each… and worked with people as individuals and in couples and families where their uniqueness and creativity were encouraged.

So the old family roles weren't as viable anymore, and the new ones hadn't been formed clearly for the younger generation regarding such a thing as egalitarian relationships, a term I am using to develop equality with couples.

I'm making *explicit* what was more *implicit* before, by "paying attention to the obvious," a famous Fritz Perls' phrase. Everyone was supporting equality in relationships, but not using a word meaning equal. So why not call these egalitarian… and spread the concept so more and more people can develop their own unique ways of being together.

CREATING OWN RELATIONSHIP STRUCTURES

So nowadays a couple must create their own roles and their own goals. With women in the workplace, couples can't rely on what their parents' and grandparents' roles were. They have to make new joint decisions if they want things to be as equal as possible.

Each relationship is unique, so each couple must *customize* their own structures, to make a win-win situation for them both. It is a lot of work, as there are no set rules that apply to everyone anymore. Hopefully, this book will be useful to those of you creating your lives together.

And that is what this book is hoping to do more efficiently and easily, and with the hope that everyone's uniqueness can be accommodated in the process. So if you are artistic, what do you need and what can you offer in your relationship. Or if you are an engineer or scientist, what is the best role for you to play. Since we are living longer than in the old days, these roles may change over time as we move into new phases in our lives.

And if there are children, elders and others in the family circle, where and how do they fit in? Lots of questions to be answered!

3.   Human Potential Movement, 1960s

"If you get the inside right, the outside will fall into place."

– Eckhart Tolle

But let's go back to the 1960s for a bit, to honor those days when the Human Potential Movement took hold. Prior to Fritz' Gestalt Therapy taking off, Abraham Maslow made a big mark on the field of counseling and psychotherapy, as well as Carl Rogers, Virginia Satir, Rollo May, Eric Berne and others. The Association for Humanistic Psychology (AHP) was formed, and they offered conferences all over the USA. Other organizations flourished as well. Group Therapy began to flourish and their conferences were well attended. Gestalt conferences began under the auspices of *The Gestalt Journal,* and later on, the Association for the Advancement of Gestalt Therapy, which is alive and well today as an international organization. And couples and family therapy began to come alive.

These teachers of new ways to work with people brought an enormous change in the fields of psychology, marriage and family counseling, social work, coaching, and education. Specialties in art therapy, music therapy, movement therapy, and psychodrama were developed.

Wilhelm Reich, MD—student of Freud's in the early 1900s and Fritz Perls' Training Analyst in Europe—fled to the USA (as had Fritz) in the 1950s, where his ideas were trashed by our government, the medical and pharmaceutical establishment, and his books were burned. He was imprisoned for issues regarding his Orgone Accumulator. He died in prison, a broken man. His daughter Eva Reich, and others worked for years to resurrect his books and ideas, many of which were stolen by the US government.

Today Reich is perceived as the "Father of Somatic Psychotherapy." Others of import during the 1960s were Elsa Gindler, Ida Rolf, Al Lowen, John Pierrakos and Charlotte Selver, all of whom influenced Fritz Perls and Gestalt Therapy in addition to Reich's work.

Along with these developments many indigenous practices surfaced and were made available to students and anyone who was interested in expanding their consciousness, a new term that was developed included Shamanism and other native ways.

The times were very exciting, and those of us on the front lines were invited to teach all over the world. Today there are Gestalt centers and institutes all over the world including places like Moscow, Cairo, and all over South America and Asia. Gestalt incorporates a lot of posture and gesture awareness, as well as body awareness in its orientation.

And since those days, as these approaches have continued to grow as separate from the establishment way of working (to varying degrees), for those of us who understand both sides of the divide, each side has influenced the other. Today there is an ongoing dialogue between practitioners of Evidence Based Therapy (EBT) and Gestalt Therapy about similar aspects within their theories.

And another emerging area is the relationship of Gestalt and Spirituality. So all of these boundaries between what is this and what is that are being explored by those well versed in their particular fields… and conferences are addressing similarities and differences as well.

And as discussed in the last chapter, the advent of Family and Couples therapy, based on Field Theory has developed alongside all of the above.

This human potential movement has been very rewarding and exciting as new ways of working and learning have been developed, not just in the United States, but all over the world. And as implied above, this movement is more about being a "Growth Model" rather than the "Medical Model" that preceded this historically: people are treated as equals rather than as subjects beneath the therapist in a hierarchy.

4.   Egalitarian Roots In Gestalt Therapy

I was fortunate to have been with Fritz Perls in the 1960s in San Francisco when he asked some of us, who had been to some of his workshops, to start an institute for Gestalt Therapy in the Bay Area. We did just that, and in 1967 we started the Gestalt Institute of San Francisco (originalgisf.com). We were the third Gestalt Institute to set up shop. The first was in NYC in 1951, and the next one was in Cleveland in 1953. I think it was just a few months after we opened, that a fourth institute opened in Los Angles with the help of James Simkin, PhD, Fritz' frequent co-leader at Esalen workshops.

Those of you familiar with Martin Buber's writings are aware of how important they were to Fritz and Laura Perls in the development of Gestalt Therapy. Besides this important way of making contact with our clients and patients, Fritz also embraced other ways to honor the egalitarian aspects of all beings.

Fritz saw himself as the "black sheep" in his family, and acknowledged he felt he was such in his wife Laura's family as well. And perhaps he was proud of this label he gave himself, realizing he was dedicated to all people being equal, and that his theories wanted to reflect this as much as possible.

I don't know if he ever wrote about this, but he constantly made reference to the importance of equality, and egalitarianism. So from my experiences with him (both in his workshops and in setting up an institute) here are the areas he stressed, which showed me his dedication to equality, personal empowerment, and egalitarianism.

I – THOU RELATIONSHIPS[1]

Developing the ability to make good contact with others is often seen as a goal in Gestalt therapy. Trainers spend a lot of time teaching students of Gestalt how to be present with one another, how to see more clearly, and how to hear more accurately,

---

1   See Bibliography for "I and Thou" by Martin Buber.

attending to the phenomenology of the moment. These are cornerstones of training at many institutes.

ENCOURAGED TO DEVELOP AN EGALITARIAN INSTITUTE

For example, when we first started the Gestalt Institute of San Francisco, Fritz encouraged us to create an egalitarian organization, a co-op or collective, where the staff of teachers all had equal power in the organization. We did this for more than 25 years, the length of time the institute was in operation. We remained a collective during the entire time, a difficult feat to be sure. Fritz also made sure to tell us that this was a suggestion, and he would not interfere by telling us what to do or not to do!

HOW OUR INSTITUTE HANDLED CONFLICT

There were many disagreements among the staff, and sometimes our staff meetings became very heated. But we were all dedicated to being an egalitarian organization. A few times we had such difficult times getting along, that we decided to hire an outside family therapist to work with us. One weekend Virginia Satir worked with us to try to clarify our dysfunctional ways. This was moderately successful as she had us line up along a continuum to see who supported whom. On another weekend we invited well-known family therapist Carl Whitaker to work with us. In both instances we realized we were a pretty hopeless *family,* and whatever help was offered we somehow didn't abide by it.

Those of you who are interested in Astrology, I had a wild awareness one day when I realized that we had five Aries men on our staff. I recall saying to those I was close to: "No wonder we are having so much trouble! We will just have to wait until they each leave to start their own centers somewhere." And slowly this happened. One went to London, another to Frankfurt, another to a hot springs in Northern California. Two, Abe Levitsky and Jack Downing, decided to stay with the rest of us, as they were dedicated to working together as a team. Eventually things began to settle down!

THE DOCTOR DOES NOT KNOW BEST

On another note, Fritz was adamant, "The doctor does not know best." On many an occasion after a person worked with Fritz in the "hot seat," Fritz asked for *feedback* from the other participants. On a number of occasions one of the participants would offer an *interpretation* of the person's work, and Fritz would immediately stop this from happening. He wanted to make sure we all understood that in Gestalt Therapy we stay away from interpretations, and instead work with our clients to the point where they can make their own interpretations, rather than someone else telling them. He said to one helpful trainee offering an interpretation, "You are doing her work for her and preventing her from discovering for herself." He made this point on many occasions. We could all see how hard it must have been for him to be a patient in Psychoanalysis, where the Analyst was interpreting his thoughts and behaviors. Perhaps this is one of the reasons he left the Analytic fold, and developed his own.

DON'T INTROJECT THE LEADER'S WAY OF WORKING, DEVELOP YOUR OWN UNIQUE STYLE

Fritz also feared that trainees in institutes would try to imitate him. He worked tirelessly during his last years to produce videos of his work before he died. However, this played into the temptation for many to imitate him, as best they could. His antidote for this was to encourage institutes and centers to bring in a number of people to do Gestalt therapy, so trainees could see many different styles. This way, he said, none of us would attempt to introject the leader's style. If we saw three or four different ways of using Gestalt, we had a better chance to find and develop *our own style*.

In San Francisco we included Laura Perls as well, as she was working on the East Coast. Every February she visited the West Coast to work with our trainees in San Francisco, and then she would fly to Los Angeles to work with their institute students.

And this is how many of us got invited to other countries to work. Every summer the Gestalt Institute of San Francisco would hold a two-week summer intensive, and sometimes two of them. We attracted a number of people from Japan and Europe, Australia and South America. When therapists from all over the world experienced Gestalt Therapy for the first or second time, they become enamored by the process, and immediately wanted to invite the leaders to their country to train a group of therapists there. This happened a lot in the 1970s and '80s and is still happening worldwide now.

The egalitarian tradition of the Gestalt Institute of San Francisco has been carried on by the Bay Area Gestalt Institute San Francisco, which refers to themselves as a Collective (www.bagisf.org). It was started by some Gestalt graduates of the California Institute of Integral Studies and members were trained by three of the original GISF staff: Lu Grey, MA; John Smolowe, MD; and Frank Rubenfeld, PhD. As far as I know, a number of other institutes are also egalitarian, but since there is no super hierarchical organization telling everyone what to do, not all are organized in the same manner. Since those of us from the 1960s in San Francisco had a lot of contact with Fritz Perls in his last days, we carried on the egalitarian principles perhaps more so than those in other parts of the world. The egalitarian principles aren't as focused on by many Gestalt writers who didn't know him personally.

As of this writing, Gestalt therapy has spread worldwide to such an extent that six months ahead of time, a joint conference sponsored by AAGT (Association for the Advancement of Gestalt Therapy) and EAGT (European Association for Gestalt Therapy), had to close registration for their conference at the end of September 2016 in Sicily with 1000 registrants!

It is truly amazing that since the first Gestalt Institute began in New York in the 1950s, today there are institutes and centers all over the globe, including such places as Japan, Taiwan, Greece, Russia, Mexico, Canada, New Zealand, Australia, and many countries in South America, as well as all over Europe. And there are a few in the Middle East, such as in Egypt.

In the 1970s, unfortunately, the term "egalitarian relationship" hadn't been used. It is my speculation that if it had, women would have become even more aware of the discrepancies in their relationships than they were at that time. The Women's Movement was a beginning in the journey towards more equality… a process that has been going on for some time.

Alyssum

a center for feminist consciousness

Due to the centuries of living in societal female roles, women have either given away their power (to men, to the establishment, to their parents and even to their children), or used it in devious, manipulative ways, thus losing much of their aliveness.

Our aim is to help women take back their power, use it fully and openly, and experience their uniqueness in the process.

We are women trained in gestalt therapy, family therapy, body work and massage and experienced in leading women's groups.

Lois Brien, Cindy Brown, Shelly Dunnigan, Pat Grosh, Lisby Mayer, Cynthia Werthman Sheldon, Anica Vesel Mander.

5. The Women's Movement of the 1970s and Its Effects on Relationships

In the 1970s when the Women's Movement began in the Bay Area, many of my clients were women seeking a more egalitarian life, even if they weren't using this exact terminology. Women wanted equality in all aspects of their lives.

In San Francisco a group of therapists organized an inexpensive program for women of all ages. It was called *Alyssum*.

ALYSSUM

This inexpensive $3 drop-in program for women held at the Gestalt Institute of San Francisco in the early 1970s, was led by two groups of women: female Gestalt therapists, and a group of "radical feminists." Over the few years of its existence, the group split along the lines mentioned above. The Gestalt women were devoted to women making the choices they felt were best for them, whereas the radical feminist women tended to discourage women from being homemakers, urging them to get all kinds of jobs in the workplace whether they were interested in them or not. They had a tendency to tell women what to do and did not ask them what they personally wanted in their lives. They were more hierarchically oriented than the Gestalt women.

The Alyssum poster is attached and says the following:

Alyssum: A center for Feminist Consciousness

Due to the centuries of living in societal female roles, women have either given away their power (to men, to the establishment, to their parents and even to their children) or used it in devious, manipulative ways, thus losing much of their aliveness.

Our aim is to help women take back their power, use it fully and openly, and experience their uniqueness in the process.

We are women trained in Gestalt therapy, family therapy, body work and massage and experienced in leading women's groups.

– Lois Brien, Cindy Brown, Shelly Dunnigan, Pat Grosh, Lisby Mayer, Cynthia Werthman Sheldon, Anica Vesel Mander

This program went on for a few years, and was meaningful to many women who were in difficult and dysfunctional relationships. Unfortunately, the term "egalitarian relationships" hadn't been used yet. It is my speculation that if it had, women would have become even more aware sooner of the discrepancies in their relationships than they were at that time. It was a beginning, however, in the journey towards more equality… a process that has been going on for some time.

All over the country articles and books started coming out about these times. Colleges and Universities were offering Women's Studies Programs. The three books listed below came from the Bay Area and discuss women, as well as psychotherapy and women during those times. Now there are many books available on this subject, written by many women and women therapists. It has been a rich field of study for many.

- *Getting Clear*, Anne Kent Rush, 1973. This book is filled with interviews of women in the Women's Movement in the San Francisco Bay Area. I appear in two interviews: one on Gestalt Therapy and one on Families and Couples.

- *Psychotherapy For Women: Treatment Toward Equality*, edited by Edna Rawlings, PhD, and Dianne K. Carter, PhD. Chapter 6: Gestalt Therapy for Women, Lois Brien PhD, and Cynthia Sheldon, MSW, pp 120-128.

- *Gestalt Awareness*, edited by Jack Downing, MD. Chapter: Women and Gestalt Awareness, pp 91-103, Lois Brien PhD and Cynthia Sheldon, MSW. 1976 Harper and Row Inc.

Although there have been some attempts at a men's movement—one started by Louis Farrakhan a number of years ago, and another called Promise Keepers, a Christian group—nothing has taken off like the Women's Movement has. I imagine now that so many men have lost their jobs, and women have changed a lot from the women of their ancestors, that another attempt to form a men's movement could happen in the near future. Books such as *Angry White Men* by Michael Kimmel, and others discuss more and more dissatisfaction among men in our world.

6. LGBT Movement

As more and more people have felt comfortable coming forth as Gay and Lesbian couples and as more states in the USA have been legalizing same sex marriages, more of these folks are now coming into therapy to get help in their relationships, as most US therapists can attest to. And this applies to the transgender folks as well.

Although it is assumed all couples have similar issues, it is my contention that same-sex couples and transgender couples don't have the historical baggage to unlock that their parents had to deal with—the traditional relationship of a man and a woman. They don't have to undo the old stereotypes of the stay-at-home Mom and the working Dad. They are more likely to assume they are equals, and may be at least one step ahead of the heterosexual couples because of this.

However, they certainly have other difficult issues to deal with, such as the prejudice against them by many people, family and friends alike.

And because we are all have psychological issues to work through to one degree or another, they too still have problems trying to get what they want from their partners by using unhealthy dynamics.

7.   When People First Meet & Once They've Been Together For Awhile

WHEN PEOPLE FIRST MEET

When people first meet one another and fall in love, they aren't into creating a relationship structure or parameters for a healthy relationship! Instead they are slowly eyeing one another and listening to one another to get an idea of what it might be like to spend a life with this person. They may ask a lot of oblique questions, hoping to have something to hang their hopes and assumptions on. And they indeed are creating a lot of assumptions during this time! "Don't ask direct questions! She might run away!" So they often become skillful at being vague and making assumptions, or trying to second guess the other by interpreting their behavior. Many play this game for a long time, and some forever. It is extremely exhausting as well.

Here are some examples:
- She must be frugal, as she only eats vegetables and grows her own fruit.
- She must want children, as she is a teacher
- She is never free on Sundays, so she must be a church goer
- He never has any money, so he must owe a lot to someone.
- Or perhaps he doesn't have a job, or he gives his money to his ex-wife for their child.

FEAR OF BEING DIRECT AND EXPLICIT

Many are afraid of ruining a potential relationship by asking too many direct questions! What if it isn't something she would agree to? What if he resents my questions? What if she thinks I'm being too presumptuous at such an early stage of our spending time together? So the vague dance goes on.

"Being direct about what I want is new to me in some ways. Since I was a young man, since I was a boy, really, I was encouraged to be direct about what I wanted to do, or what I wanted to be. But being direct about what I want emotionally, what I desire relationally, or what I want from myself and for myself emotionally — I don't recall learning how to do that.

"Now in my mid 40s, thanks to attending Cyndy's Egalitarian Relationship workshops, I have discovered that being direct (with myself, and with others) is the path to authenticity. In my family of origin, being direct about 'what you wanted' was seen as being pushy, or self-centered, and far from a virtue. Over time, sarcasm, raised eye-brows, gossip and conversations about work filled the void created by our family's commitment to not being direct about emotional matters.

"I now believe mutual directness is essential, and that intimacy without emotional directness is a pathway to unnecessary resentments, disappointments, and other forms of interpersonal drama, whereas directness coupled with good will allows hurts and upsets to be expressed and moved through, and the intimacy deepened."

– Alex, Seattle

This cautiousness can also lead to: "He never asks me any questions about myself. He must not be interested, or he is too self-centered." A number of men in my practice have told me when this issue came up, "I don't ask her questions, as I'd be intruding. She'll tell me if she wants to or when she is ready." This often is not acceptable to their lady friends!

My high school boyfriend told me (many years later) that my being explicit with him about wanting children, and a home with a white picket fence, "freaked him out." Being secretive, he didn't tell me this until 30 years later! We never lived together or married, but kept in contact over the years. And now 65 years later in reviewing our lives, he was the one who married, had kids, and literally lived in a house with a white picket fence! I lost interest in wanting these things. I guess the moral of this story is that one never knows for sure what one will think or feel later on in life, so being explicit about future wants may be a futile exercise!

Often we assume that if someone says they want 12 kids, that want will be there forever. On the other hand, we want our partner to believe that this is true for us *now,* and maybe in five years it won't be the case. Every time we use the words 'want' or 'hope' or 'desire', we are talking about the future. "Tomorrow I want…, next year I want…, in five years I hope to be… ." We often change our minds as we interact with life over time, but once we've said what we want, our partner may forget about the effects of our lives changing over time.

Unlike many others, being vague wasn't the case when I met my husband to be. We met in Ann Arbor at a student conference in the 1950s, and stayed up all one summer night by a lake discussing what we wanted in our futures. He was very direct with me saying that if we got together he didn't want to have to compete with me for jobs since we were both in the same field, sociology. Later on, after he knew me better, he hoped I would become a therapist, as he thought I'd be good at that… and much to my surprise I ended up doing that. And it was definitely for my best.

Although my husband was very direct with me, he was not in any way insinuating he and I would be together. It was five or six years later that we married.

EXPERIMENT
If you are in a new relationship, list what assumptions you are making.

1. **Are you being vague?**
2. **Are you afraid to share certain things?**
3. **Are you afraid to ask questions of him or her?**

ONCE YOU'VE BEEN TOGETHER FOR SOME TIME

So once you've managed to decide to live together, you probably know one another fairly well. You think you do, at any rate, until you finally go running and screaming to a therapist who asks you many questions about you and your partner, questions you have no answers to! So you actually may not know your partner very well at all!

The therapist might ask you:
- What is your partner's religious or spiritual orientation?
- How many times has he or she been married?
- What were the problems in those relationships?
- Have you met his family of origin or siblings or children?
- Do you know her work history and educational background?
- Has he ever done anything illegal?
- Has she gotten caught and what were the consequences?
- Has he or she been sick, troubled, or seen a therapist before?

Many of these questions partners can't answer about their loved one!

EXPERIMENTS

1. *One suggestion I make to couples who have been together a while is to go out on a date... and pretend they've just met. Find out some things about your partner that you don't know, such as "what was one of your most embarrassing moments," or "tell me about your childhood sweetheart," or "how do you understand why your last marriage fell apart," or "do you owe anyone any money?" It is okay for you to be curious, especially if you might end up spending the rest of your lives together!*

2. *And you might also want to ask your partner how he or she feels about you asking so many questions.*

3. *Encourage both of you to do so if you really want to know... and if you don't, well maybe this isn't the relationship you thought it would be!*

And remember, you don't have to answer every question you are asked.

8.   The Many Hierarchies in Our Lives

"Don't walk in front of me… I may not follow. Don't walk behind me…
I may not lead. Walk beside me… just be my friend."

– Albert Camus

Let's look at all of the hierarchies in our lives. Let's start at the time we were born: an infant being taken care of by one or several adults. Those adults told us what we could do and what we couldn't do. Do you remember some of those infant times and some of the teachings of the elders in your lives?

Next we became students in the hierarchies of schools we attended. Again, we were subjects of these folks who were above us in the pecking order, teaching us many things as we slowly moved towards adulthood.

And next many of us became employees at the behest of employers. Most of us have had at least one or many experiences being an employee, again beholden to our bosses, and the companies they represented.

The first job, a summer job, I had was with Reader's Digest, *a fairly large company in those days! It was in my home town. This was back in about 1951 or '52 when I was a junior or senior in high school. I recall receiving letters for those who were registered for something* Reader's Digest *offered every now and then. It was a book that had summaries of four or five novels in it, that had been rewritten for* Reader's Digest. *We handled the subscriptions to these books. I worked in the file section. One day I got a letter inviting* Reader's Digest *to visit a Nudist colony somewhere in New Jersey! Well, this became the talk of the department for the rest of the summer while I worked there! This was my first job in a hierarchical organization, and I don't recall ever having to meet my boss, or deal with any issues around its structure! And I was never ordered, at age 18, to visit the Nudist colony! And it was an interesting first job in the adult world of hierarchies.*

Probably after experiencing all three of these roles in our lives—child, student, employee—we then became a parent, a teacher and an employer, where we ruled over those under us in the pecking order.

My favorite memory was when I was about 12, sitting in the back seat of the family car, next to my 8-year-old brother. He was talking on and on about how he was learning all about democracy in school. He then posed the 64,000 dollar question to our parents: "Why can't we have democracy at home?" At this point our German mother turned around, flung the back of her hand at my brother and somewhat playfully screamed, "There will be no democracy in this family!" End of story!

I find it curious that I recall this memory more than so many, and I wonder what that is all about. I do know I have always been a fighter for everyone's equal rights. Here was an early example of learning something about this important value in my own family.

Another memory is when I was 13, and went to a local Quaker Meeting with my close friends. It was in 1947. There were probably about 15 young folks in the Sunday School run by the mother of a friend of mine, Dorothy Williams. Mrs. Williams, as we called her then, was busy teaching us about Jesus, while a new local synagogue was on the drawing boards to be built in nearby Mt. Kisco. All the local churches were invited to make a contribution. At our local Quaker Meeting, the elders had voted the idea down as they could not reach consensus, so they did not participate in this contribution—and I imagined most of the churches and religious organizations in this area had participated.

Now Mrs. Williams had the urge to rebel, and she took all 15 of us in the Sunday School and we stormed out of the building in protest. We quit! We were protesting the fact that our Quaker Meeting had refused to participate with a contribution to the new Synagogue. Mrs. Williams had said that since she was teaching us about Jesus, who was a Jew, she could not continue teaching if this Quaker Meeting did not honor Judaism. So this was my first protest! Thank you, Mrs. Williams!

Although the Quaker Meeting was a consensus-driven egalitarian organization, which I didn't appreciate until I was much older, I am very proud to have had that opportunity at such a young age to protest. During this time I attended Quaker Quarterly Meetings in a nearby small town, and I recall those as being egalitarian as we conducted business sessions. For what, I don't recall. But there I was being trained into the wonders of an egalitarian organization, which I would later see as a blessing in disguise, as there are so few of them in the world.

As you do this experiment below, realize how many hierarchies there are, one on top of the other into infinity it seems. While writing this in mid-2016, as USA elections are in the news daily, the world looks very grim now for many Americans. Honoring our uniqueness as individuals, which many of us grew up believing was part of growing up in a democratic society, looks further and further away as a reachable goal. Many of us who have been fighting for our own democratic rights, as well as for those of others, are surely wondering what is and has been happening. And we are wondering if it is it possible to change the course of history at this point.

EXPERIMENTS

1. **Review your life; note all of the hierarchies you've been part of.**
2. **Ask yourself how you felt as a subject in each of them, both as the one at the bottom of the ladder, as well as being the parent, teacher or boss on occasion.**
3. **Share with your partners and friends if you so desire.**

9.   A Global Impasse: Transition Time

It certainly isn't new information that more and more people are taking to the streets worldwide to protest the lack of egalitarian societies in which they live. People are demanding freedom all over the globe, in all sorts of situations: in the way their country is run politically, in organizations, and in relationships. You hear shouts of Freedom! Equality! Fairness! Democracy!

So Revolution is in the air on all of these levels in the United States and abroad. In some way you can say we are all in a time of transition, from one paradigm of how to live our lives, to another, which may not be clear to us yet.

In Gestalt lingo this dynamic is often referred to as ***the impasse***. It is as if we've sailed away from the shore where we knew what to expect in our lives, and we haven't landed on the opposite shore in the new life we may be moving towards. We are floating along the river in between these two poles: the past and the future.

As Gestalt folks often say, "Don't Push the River, It Flows by Itself." Be aware and alert, and see what emerges next on this journey to what is happening to all of us.

Section C

Words & Concepts

1. New Twists on Important Words and Concepts

1. New Twists on Important Words and Concepts

ACCEPTANCE

This word does not mean that I accept everything that is going on in my life and the world in general. It means I accept what I am experiencing in the moment. Once I accept where I am in the moment, I usually take a deep breath automatically, or sigh. This brings me into alignment as my words and my body and my being are saying the same thing. I am not trying to be somewhere where I am not! *I am here now.* I accept that. I may not like it, but I accept it... for *this* moment. This act of here and now acceptance allows me to be open to whatever might emerge on my mind's screen in the next moment. For example:

> *I accept that at this moment I am very tired, and my eyes are burning. And now, my eyes feel a little better as I acknowledge this moment. I breathe more fully. Now I experience a deeper tiredness. I accept this right now. I think I will finally stop writing and go to bed! I do not want to try to be awake when I am not!*

Thank you to Arnold Beisser, MD, who developed this idea as the Paradoxical Theory of Change, an important concept in Gestalt Therapy.

FORGIVENESS

I've been hearing this word for so many years, and I've never liked it. It reeks of hierarchy to me. Let me explain why. Who is the one forgiving who for doing what? This word assumes someone has done something wrong, or bad, to need some kind of forgiveness. Here is an example:

> *He: I forgive you for forgetting our meeting yesterday.*

> *She: Did I do something wrong to merit your holier-than-though forgiveness? I don't want your forgiveness. I didn't do anything wrong. And furthermore you*

assumed I did do something wrong without asking me what happened. That was very presumptuous of you!

It smacks of hierarchy, which doesn't bode well for an increasingly egalitarian society, in spite of the ruling elite. And it implies almost a religiosity, like God is working through you to forgive me for the terrible thing you think I did to you!

FREEDOM

This word is bandied around all the time, particularly on the news. People everywhere want freedom. And in the USA the Conservatives scream it, and the Liberals scream it as well. What it sounds like, without putting it into some understandable context, is that we are all spoiled and want our own way and the hell with everyone else. The Republicans scream this whenever a Democrat wants to help others. To me it is a word which can mask hierarchy, and is used to manipulate the masses into following them, because who doesn't want freedom.

HIERARCHY

This word is all about who is on top and who is on the bottom and who is in between. It is a triangle with the powerful at the top, ruling whomever is under them. There is no equality here. Most of us have lived within one hierarchy or another most of our lives, either at the bottom with a ruler on top, or maybe we made it to the top of a pyramid somewhere along the line.

AUTHORITY

There are many kinds of authority. There is the boss, the bully, the benevolent one. In all cases they can hire or fire us, suspend us from school, or punish us. We have no power. If we have to have such a being above us, most of us would prefer a benevolent one. I suspect the problem with this person, is that many people don't realize they aren't equal to him or her, who still has the final say-so.

EQUALITY

Not much new to add to this word. We all want it, except those in power! There are some wonderful photos going around on the internet of individual animals and birds with the caption under it saying, "I am someone." They are most touching, and remind us that this desire for equality is within the soul of all of us, as many believe.

RESISTANCE

This word is used a lot in psychotherapy. To me it implies that a client is resistant to whatever the therapist is suggesting, interpreting, or offering. It sounds like the therapist is blaming the client for not going along with her or him, as after all, "the doctor knows best." And to resist is to show some kind of neurotic dynamic. Could it simply be that the client *doesn't like being told what is true or not true*, and the therapist's comments might not fit? Again this smacks of hierarchy, not equality.

PROTECTION

I prefer to sense that a client who doesn't agree with a therapist might find ways to protect himself if he can't speak up directly to the therapist. So rather than calling these behaviors resistance, I refer to them as protections. Clients, like everyone else, usually don't like being told what to do or think or feel. Sometimes therapists think they know what is best for us, and then we need to protect against such arrogance, even if "it is for our own good."

COOPERATIVE

As both a noun and a verb. As an adjective, this word implies that two people work together towards something such as a relationship. They cooperate with one another; they are co-operative. As a noun their relationship structure could be seen as a co-operative, where they are both the CEOs of their home and life together.

GIVING / RECEIVING

Here is a polarizing dynamic. I *give*, you *take* (or receive), but you can already hear the slant by using the word *take*—givers are good guys; takers are bad guys. Many feel self righteous when they "give" to the poor. The rich get lots of kudos when they give millions to non-profit organizations. This dynamic allows many to feel good that they are doing something to help *the other*, who is not one of them.

The receiver is often perceived as the "taker." And takers are considered dependent on others and on society. They are often disrespected and not considered one of the *others*, who are more responsible.

This dynamic is at the basis of the Democratic and Republican parties: the Republicans believe poor people are *takers* and the government should not have any programs which help them. Democrats believe their democratic socialistic society is structured to help everyone in many ways, often by giving incentives to people to take more responsibility for their lives.

A new paradigm is needed for these two words. A *gives* B a copy of his book to help her in some way. The word 'gives' implies a 'taking away from' A, and helping B. This is a hierarchical dynamic. I'm above you, feeling helpful to you; you are needy and therefore, below me.

If we see it as A *wanting* B to have a copy of his book, we can understand that this is for A, perhaps more than it is for B. B may or may not want the book. If B enjoys the book, both have been part of this sharing, a more egalitarian way of perceiving the situation.

> *I spend a lot of time sending emails to people about health issues and animals, because I like sharing this information. I do not experience myself as giving to them. I could chose to see things that way, but if I did I probably would be resentful if they didn't give me something back. I am not giving these emails to them to feel good about myself being helpful to others. It is much more personal than all of the above: I enjoy doing it. It is fun for me. I giggle and get a kick out of all the photos I send around.*

NEED / WANT

Gestalt co-founder Fritz Perls had strong opinions and feelings about these two words. Believing we all should be responsible for ourselves, he felt the word *need* implied a dependency on others, a neediness. Other than the basic physiological needs of life such as shelter, food, and water, he preferred the word *want* to describe all other desires. Thus, whenever a trainee would use the word *need* referring to love or caring, he would see this as a manipulation, and ask the person to change the word *need* to *want*.

> *Jasmine: I need my boyfriend to hold and love me, and he always withdraws when I ask him.*
>
> *Therapist: Say the same sentence again, and substitute the word want for need.*
>
> *Jasmine: I want my boyfriend to hold and love me, and he always withdraws when I ask him.*
>
> *Therapist: How do the two sentences sound to you? What are you aware of?*
>
> *Jasmine: When I use the word 'want' I don't sound so needy, or demanding. Maybe that turns him off, or scares him. I don't mean it that way. I'll try changing the word and see what happens.*

She went on to say that she sounded like she was whining when she used the word *need,* and she experienced herself as trying to get something from her boyfriend and the therapist when she used this word, like she was manipulating them. When she used the word *want* she felt more like an adult standing on her own two feet.

CONCLUDING / GENERALIZING / THEORIZING

Anyone who has been to school in the past hundred years, at least in the USA, has had a lot of experience and training in school to make conclusions, generalizations and even theories. We've been graded on how well we can do this. Unfortunately many of us have grown into adults using this way of speaking more frequently than not. *This is my theory right now!* And what is so often the case, is that we rarely back up our generalizations with some data or observable phenomena.

Instead, many began seeing their reality in *concepts*. They were one step removed from their full experience. An example is the word FEAR.

It is a concept: having fear. Sometimes it is a verb. "I fear going home by myself." Many in the USA say, "Don't let yourself go into fear." As a therapist I ask clients who exclaim that they are afraid, to tell me where in their bodies they are feeling fear right now, and to describe this experience in more detail. Most cannot do this, as they aren't feeling it. They are thinking it. It is just a concept to them, that they've superimposed on a situation.

Gestalt therapy has emphasized how important it is to go into the specifics, to become aware of the phenomena that led to the generalization. What did I see, hear, smell, taste or sense when I said I was afraid? What sensations and feelings did I have at that time?

"Lose your mind and come to your senses," the founders used to say. Be in touch with your whole being, not just the concepts you are *thinking*. People don't sound authentic when they speak in concepts.

What a disservice education has been to teach us, unwittingly, I imagine, how to ignore our full experience—and to live in our heads with all the concepts and theories we can come up with. We miss a lot of actual life when we do this so often and so regularly.

MANIPULATION: BEING DIRECT AND CLEAR

From a Gestalt point of view, manipulation is seen as an attempt to get what we want through indirect means, which we think will be more effective than asking directly for whatever we want. Children, who have no power when they are little, find ways to hopefully convince their parents to give them what they want by using approaches such as charm, acting sick, rebelling, crying, and raging. And often these ways are carried into adulthood, especially if they worked well when we were little.

To ask as an adult, by being clear and direct, puts us in the situation of possibly being told *no*. To Fritz Perls, being able to hear the word *no* is a sign of being a healthy adult, whereas manipulation is seen as a childish way to con the authority into giving them what they want so they can avoid hearing no. Also, being direct and clear is a sign of taking responsibility for our desires.

POSITIVE / NEGATIVE

If you begin to listen to peoples' conversation, including those of your friends, chances are you will hear the words **positive** or **negative** a lot. From a Gestalt orientation, both of these words are generalizations that people make about something they are talking about to someone else. They are *evaluating* whatever they are talking about, and giving them one of these two labels.

Constant evaluation is being done by many of us. I don't think most people are aware of how often they evaluate what they are thinking, saying, doing, feeling, and so forth. For many of us it is constant!

> *"Don't say that; you're being negative. Don't go there.*
> *You create your own reality!"*

How often have you caught yourself evaluating by using one of these two words? And does your partner use them as well? What is it about us that we have to evaluate so much all the time. I know we got good grades in school for doing so! But I don't think anyone expected us to use these words so often.

Our normal greeting in the USA is: "Hello, how are you?" This invites us to go into our heads to evaluate how we are, over and over and over again, sometimes all day long! And then, if we say we aren't well or we are having a bad day, we might hear from them: "Don't go there, you are being negative!"

There is an important sociological book that deals somewhat with this phenomenon called *Bright-Sided: How The Relentless Promotion of Positive Thinking Has Undermined America*, by Barbara Ehrenreich (Holt Books, NY, 2009). Take a look at this when you have time. It can help keep us in balance.

EGALITARIAN RELATIONSHIP

Two people who claim they are a couple, or partners, or lovers, who decide together the way they want to organize and live their lives. This does not necessarily mean they have to do everything 50-50. They just have to agree. There may be some items that are non-negotiable, which both can say they insist on. And with these items, it is up to the other to agree or not.

EGALITARIAN

(from French *égalitaire*, from *égalité*, equality, from Latin *aequālitās*, *aequālis*, equal)

This word is an adjective, meaning: affirming, promoting, or characterized by a belief in equal political, economic, social, and civil rights for all people.

It does not include the personal, but I use it in this new way about relationships, as I think it fits perfectly.

RELATIONSHIP

(re·la·tion·ship (rĭ-lā'shən-shĭp')

This word is a noun meaning: The condition or fact of being related; connection or association.

Connection by blood or marriage; kinship. A particular type of connection existing between people related to or having dealings with each other: has a close relationship with his siblings. A romantic or sexual involvement.

Section D

Creating an Egalitarian Relationship Structure

1. Creating an Egalitarian Relationship Structure

1.   Creating an Egalitarian Relationship Structure

FIVE MAIN AREAS OF LIFE:
HEALTH, RELATIONSHIPS & FAMILY, SPIRITUALITY, FINANCES, CAREERS

Over the past few years I've held experiential classes on the theme of this book. **An egalitarian relationship is one in which both parties decide together** the issues all couples have to deal with when they live together. In addition to a wonderful romantic connection, they are also working as a co-creative team running a small co-operative business—their household.

Deciding together doesn't necessarily mean everything has to be divided 50-50! It can include: agreeing that she is the main breadwinner, dividing the finances on a percentage basis or not, taking separate vacations on occasion, and each having their own private space if feasible. There are no *shoulds* about what they decide, only that they *decide and agree together*. And obviously couples can't decide every minute detail about everything so they may decide that one person is the boss of the kitchen, and so forth.

In my classes on this topic, participants break up into pairs, preferably with someone other than their partner, to experiment with creating an egalitarian structure that will meet the needs of both parties. I do this exercise in the beginning of the class and at the end, giving participants an opportunity to experience creating such a structure with a couple of people before trying it with their partners. Also, on occasion, the men become women and the women become men, to get a feel for what it is like to see things from the point of view of the opposite sex. Same sex couples are also role played on occasion.

AREAS OF AGREEMENT

In the beginning the participants focus on those items they can come to agreement on, avoiding disagreement, negotiation or compromise. There is some excitement doing this process and almost all of them reported new awarenesses about themselves, their partners, and their parents' relationship.

AREAS OF DISAGREEMENT

Next I ask them to find the areas of disagreement, and how they managed to slip by these. Many glossed over these areas and felt uncomfortable disagreeing until I gave them permission to do so with gusto. Again the room was filled with excitement, as some disagreed unlike they had ever done before. Again, new awarenesses popped up as they shared their experiences with one another.

When asked what she felt about uninvited guests, she became suddenly mum! She hadn't thought of this and realized how nervous she was to tell her fairly new partner that this would be very hard for her to go along with. She couldn't imagine her partner's family members thinking it was okay to drop in whenever they felt like it.

* * *

Years ago, a couple I was working with asked me to go to their house to see the struggle they were having decorating their home by co-mingling his African mask collection with her grandmother's lace collection! Luckily they had a sense of humor about this, so we had a lot of laughs as we draped lace over a devilish looking mask. They found a way to work things out by putting them in two small rooms, neither of which was the main living room.

CREATIVE COMPROMISE

Some creative couples who haven't been able to agree on some aspects of living together, decided to live next door to one another or nearby; or if neither in a couple are willing to quit their job to live with the other, they might decide to live in separate communities, often far from one another. I knew one couple who lived apart for years, at each end of California. Another couple lived 3000 miles apart, one on each coast of the USA.

CONTENT VERSUS PROCESS

Most of the struggles couples experience have little to do with the *content* of their arguments, such as which movie do we go see tonight, who lost the keys. But rather they struggle with the *process* between them and how they communicate or don't communicate well with one another, where they don't follow egalitarian principles of fairness, consideration of one another, good will for themselves and their partners.

Often when one gets his or her way more than the other, the other capitulates to avoid conflict, and ends up resenting the other. And naturally, over time, this has a disastrous effect on the relationship.

By dealing with the *content* of what needs deciding, the couple can learn about their *process* and find ways to "do it better." Many will say they argue about such *stupid things* as how to squeeze the toothpaste or how to clean the stove. I assure them that all arguments are important, as they reveal the *process* of how they deal with things, which occur in many situations, including big decisions.

UNILATERAL DECISIONS

Everyone who participated in the classes wanted an egalitarian relationship and most had parts of one, but many areas they'd overlooked. This surprised a lot of the participants. Seeing the issues they didn't decide in an egalitarian manner helped explain some of their struggles with one another. For example, they held resentments towards the one who made *unilateral decisions*. In the end, many were relieved to understand themselves and their partner better.

CONCRETE ITEMS

Now let's look at many of these ideas more specifically. Here is a list of the items most discussed in creating an egalitarian structure during the classes.

With many of these, people often, without awareness, assume *everyone* does things like they do, or like their parents did. But, assumptions are tickets for wrong expectations, and wrong expectations are juice for conflicts! So, be aware of the expectations you are assuming. Ask yourself and your partner to consider these areas and what is important to you about them.

1. MOVING INTO ONE PERSON'S RENTAL OR HOME

Often it is a ticket for catastrophe if one moves into another's space without discussing the implications first. One person's decor might not suit the other. The space needs, cleanliness practices, where to put the partner's things may also come into play here. Question to ask each other: "How open are you to co-mingling your things together, and how can you do it with the least conflict? Can you easily change the label of *my* place or *your* place to *our* place."

By moving into a new place together, a neutral *our place*, is often easier for both parties. This way you can decide together which place to rent, and co-create the way you want to use the space. For example, do you each want to have a separate office or room to do your meditating, projects, writing, watching computer or TV programs the other isn't interested in?

2. OWNING YOUR LIVING SPACE

It is perhaps best if both can co-own equally. This assures they each have an equal say about the condo or house, and can decide if and when to sell it or what to spend money on if they plan to fix it up, and so forth. Legal agreements can be made to meet the egalitarian needs of each to some extent. For example: if he makes less money than her, they can decide if he is half owner, even if he only can afford a third of the place and pays a third of the mortgage. If this isn't possible, and one of the pair has to be the full owner, this again is a catastrophe waiting to happen. She has the power to sell, to spend monies fixing it up the way she wants to. Egalitarian control of the house or condo doesn't work here, and it is a breeding ground for resentments on his part. If he hides his resentments they'll probably slip out somehow. He might begin by being sarcastic towards her, pulling away from her emotionally, becoming passive aggressive with her, and so on.

3. FINANCES
- Do you co-mingle your monies, have separate accounts, or do a little of each?
- If one of the couple is in debt, how will you handle it?
- How do you deal with one person making a lot more money than the other?
- Story from *MS Magazine* in the 1970s, during the beginning of the Women's Movement:

An unhappy stay-at-home mother with three young children and a husband who made a good living, took things into her own hands as the Women's Movement sparked her courage. She wrote down everything she did every day for a month, figured out how much each thing she did was worth financially, and then presented her husband with a bill, including the time it took her to determine the cost. She checked with her husband and others as to how much to charge him for such things as: child development expert, taxi driver, cook, house cleaner, running errands for husband, hiring gardener, being the chief chef, family vacation planner and organizer, and so on!

4. HOME RESPONSIBILITIES
How do you divide up the work around the house, yard, garage, or do you hire or barter some or all of it?

5. VEHICLES
Who is responsible for what with each vehicle?

6. HEALTH AND HEALTHCARE
Do you both have healthcare? Are you okay with what you each have? One may have better healthcare than the other, which can lead to problems. Ask what you might consider doing if there are problems in this area? For example, one of you might prefer alternative medicine, which often is not covered by health insurance.

7. PETS
Who is responsible for feeding, walking, and care-taking pets? Who would get which pet if the couple separates.

8. CHILDREN AND OTHERS WHO LIVE WITH YOU
The minute children come on the scene, the family becomes hierarchical, although the couple can maintain *their* egalitarian relationship. If relatives, friends, children from other marriages join your family, it would help if you (the couple) discussed at length how to handle decisions with the additional people. You *both* are still the head of the family unless in some way others buy into the structure financially and otherwise. This takes good and careful negotiating. As long as the couple is in charge of who can live there or not, this is a hierarchy, and the couple *together* can ask others to leave or invite them to stay.

9. TIME TOGETHER AND TIME APART
Do you value vacations? Together? Separate? Consider the idea that visiting family might not be a vacation, no matter how wonderful they are. Remember when couples are away from one another, they miss each other! Experiment and take time off from one another on occasion!

10. USE OF TECHNOLOGY
- Who gets to watch TV if it is in the main room?
- If you are talking together, is it okay to interrupt to answer cell or text?
- If you text or call, how much time do you wait before being concerned, angry...
- How soon after texting do you *expect* your partner to respond?

11. INVITED AND UNINVITED GUESTS
This item is often forgotten about, but very important. Some people are very comfortable

having people drop-in, whereas others want people to call first. If a couple doesn't have the same take on this one, it is very important that they find a way to negotiate this.

12. USE OF MIND-ALTERING SUBSTANCES
A big issue is whether both or either are regular users of alcohol, psychedelics, over-the-counter drugs, hardcore drugs, prescription drugs, marijuana. This one is crucial because if one of you is in an altered state and the other one isn't, the lack of a connection can be upsetting to one or both of you. As you know, you can't expect to be on the same wave length if one is using and the other one isn't. Lots of negotiation around this one may be needed.

13. SPIRITUALITY AND RELIGION
In the old days, 60 years ago perhaps, it was common for people to never discuss religion or politics. In keeping with the theme of egalitarian relationships, I encourage couples to discuss their views to see if they are okay with living with possible differences in this area of religion or spirituality.

14. POLITICS
It is always good to discuss, along with any other taboo subject as well. "How do you feel if we are not members of the same or any political party?"

15. SEXUAL PREFERENCES AND PRACTICES
Again, it is always important to be able to discuss this issue, as individuals may have strong feelings about certain practices. How important is sex to you? How often?

16. FOOD
Discussing when you like to eat, what you like to eat, and where you like to eat can be a most fruitful discussion—so that you understand cooking arrangements as well as how,

what and where to purchase what you love to eat. Who pays for a type of food one of you doesn't want to eat?

NON-NEGOTIABLES

Be aware of what issues seem non-negotiable to you. Discuss it with your partner. This item could become negotiable once you understand one another better.

> *Don was friendly with his ex-wife and wanted to meet monthly while in his new relationship, but his current wife was having trouble with this request. After discussing it for awhile, Don stopped seeing his ex-wife. Six months later his current partner was okay with this idea; she just needed some time to get to know him better.*

CONTACT WITHDRAWAL RHYTHM

See Chapter F4 on this theme. Everyone may have a different rhythm of contact and withdrawal. There is no good or bad or right or wrong way for how much time we want to be in contact with the other. As I indicate in the chapter on this theme, we each have our own rhythm once we become aware of it. This could be in conflict with our partner's rhythm. For example: some are night owls and love to go to late movies, bars or night clubs, whereas the other may like to climb into bed with a good book early and avoid all of the nighttime activity. Obviously folks need to come to some kind of compromise on these differences if they have the time and money for them!

CREATE SEPARATE TIME TO DISCUSS ISSUES

- Learn techniques to deal with differences and sharing them with one another. Being open to listening to your partner's ideas *fully* to understand where the other is coming from, usually helps couples a lot. At least they feel understood when this happens, even if it doesn't solve the dilemma.
- Brainstorming is where you put all the ideas about a topic on the table. No one is

allowed to find fault with any until all ideas are on the table.

- Remember that once you have a structure in place, one or both of you may want to change things. Over time expect changes, as change is the one constant in life!

FUN TIMES TOGETHER

This is important for your mental, social and intimate health! Many couples forget to create these times together with the feeling they are too busy. We all know how important this one is.

HOW SPEEDY OR SLOW ARE EACH OF YOU

Lots of couples struggle with this theme! Bernadette agrees she is responsible for doing the dishes, but doesn't do it as quickly as Stephannie wishes her to. This often leads to one person's rhythm being very different than the other's. Often one will be the complainer and the other the one complained about, over and over. This can set up a very unhealthy dynamic unless the couple can talk about this and resolve it.

> *"You are too slow; you procrastinate! I know our rhythms are different in terms of getting things done, but my way is more efficient and better. You should do something to speed up and finish what you start. You drive me crazy with a frequently half cleaned up kitchen!"*

Some couples find ways to take care of this by accepting each other's timing and so on. Others can't come to agreement. I'll cover what to do if couples can't negotiate or compromise in a later chapter.

So this is a partial list of things we have talked about in the classes. Many new awarenesses occurred when the twosomes in the class changed gender roles, so they could get a better idea how the other might feel. This was a big plus for many of the couples.

There may be many issues and concerns I've left out, but this is probably a good list to begin structuring or restructuring your relationship.

Section E

Healthy Relationships

1. **Healthy Egalitarian Relationships**

2. **Being Present**

3. **Dealing Well With Conflict**

4. **Curiosity**

1. Healthy Egalitarian Relationships

"But let there be spaces in your togetherness and let the winds of the heavens dance between you. Love one another but make not a bond of love: let it rather be a moving sea between the shores of your souls."

– Khalil Gibran

I'm always a little nervous discussing *healthy people & healthy relationships,* as readers are often looking for a new set of "shoulds" to live by. Then they end up having more things about which to criticize themselves and their partners, and I certainly don't want to contribute to that. These ideas need to be said to help *guide* us rather than set up new *rules* to live by. Some of these may not fit everyone, so they all need to be taken with a grain of salt.

HISTORICAL NOTE

Most couples sense early on in their relationship whether their values are similar or not. However, as you all know, many of us ignore our 'senses' when we fall in love, only to find they appear after the 'honeymoon' is over! I often ask couples when they knew certain things would come up as issues between them. What most of them said was "the first or second time we got together!" I found this to be quite a powerful awareness on the part of so many. And it was true in my own case as well.

In previous eras there was a slogan in the USA: "Never talk about politics or religion," meaning many couples had differences in these areas, and many learned to accept their differences in those days although it meant they kept a piece of themselves out of their relationships, which probably diminished their connection with one another to some degree.

1. EMOTIONALLY HEALTHY PEOPLE ARE CONGRUENT AND ALIGNED

This means their words, actions, demeanor, all say the same thing. In a larger context Navajos, with whom I worked for 10 years, would say they are aligned with Mother Earth and Father Sky. Their different aspects and qualities are not fighting with one another. All aspects are on the same page, so to speak. It also can mean someone is authentic and genuine.

2. EMOTIONALLY HEALTHY PEOPLE WANT TO CONTRIBUTE AND RECEIVE SUPPORT FROM THEIR COMMUNITIES AND THE LARGER SOCIETY

I'm not so sure this is the case today, at least in the USA. Many want to find others whom they can share all of their interests and beliefs with, so that they don't hide parts of themselves and diminish their connection with one another. Since many are best friends with their partners now, at least before things go badly between them, there is a tendency to wish for commonality in as many areas as possible. The family is not just for procreation to have more hands to help the family survive as was true in the old days. People partner to create family and community with strong needs for friendship, love and respect.

Perhaps in the USA, which has often been labeled as having a John Wayne mentality, meaning everybody does his own thing, community hasn't been that important. And the Industrialization Age brought with it mobility, where families and couples were and still are transferred to companies all over the map, disrupting any kind of deep community connections which often take time to develop.

And now this seems to be changing. More and more people are looking for community. Look at the growing interest in sharing space together, not *just* for financial reasons, such as living in co-operative housing, retirement homes, co-housing communities, back to the land communities, but also growing local gatherings for special interests and the newly emerging on-line communities. Even within the Gestalt Therapy world, some of us are working towards more like-minded communities of people who are open to learning about ourselves, and becoming more aware. Erv Polster, PhD, Gestalt Therapist Emeritus, has been developing this idea for many years and recently has written a couple of books on the subject.

One of the things I've done for years when working with couples who are new to the area or somewhat isolated, is to encourage them to have a common project together, such as a hobby, a small business, a religious or spiritual pursuit, volunteering together, giving money to a cause, taking a class together, enjoying a sport together, and so on. This way they are giving something to a cause greater then themselves often in their community and they are getting to know like minded others in their areas of interest.

3. EMOTIONALLY HEALTHY PEOPLE CAN BE TRUTHFUL, CLEAR AND DIRECT

a. Learning to be direct, truthful and clear isn't easy for many of us. The English language for starters is often vague. I learned this on the Navajo Reservation, when the Navajos would make fun of our vagueness. Their language, which I wish I could speak, is much clearer. They say what they mean, and they mean what they say.

b. Being direct is rude in some cultures. In some there is no word for 'no'.

One summer years ago when I lived in a village in Mexico with the Quakers, I learned a little conversational Spanish. I was taught not to use the word 'no'. If I meant no, I was to say yes (si') and wag my finger sideways to indicate the no part of the communication!

c. Qualifiers—often used to soften the blow of what we want to say—more often confuse the listener who is trying to understand us.

For example: I sort of *would like us to visit my parents tonight, even though I know you* probably *aren't too eager to do this.*

d. Being Truthful is very subjective. There is no way we could be truthful all of the time about everything. There isn't enough time in the day! Plus we often weigh the hurtfulness of our truth telling with the value of it. This is often a difficult thing to discern. Some people tell the truth to their partner to assuage their own guilt. They expect their partner to be pleased to hear the truth, and aren't sensitive to the effect of what they are saying might have on him or her.

e. Note that I said *can be* direct, meaning if the person deems it would be wise to be so. This is not a *should*. There are many times when it might seem best not to be direct.

4. EMOTIONALLY HEALTHY PEOPLE CAN OFTEN FIND CREATIVE WAYS TO WORK THINGS OUT WITH THEIR PARTNER

It may not be necessary to have long discussions and time for each to fully explain themselves. Everyone isn't wired to do this. Some definitely are. A few years ago I worked with a couple where one wanted the long conversations and the other didn't. Eventually they discovered that if one of them felt hurt about something, they could just say "Ouch!" And the other would get it and she might say back "Oops, I'm sorry!" And this could be the end of this conversation. They might not need a 3 hour evaluation and explanation of what each saw the other doing and how that affected each of them. And some people prefer this approach! There is no right and wrong.

If someone is talking a lot, rather than accusing her of such, raise your hand and tell her "my turn" in a nonjudgmental light manner.

Most of us wait until things go badly before we seek help or try to find new ways of being and working together. There may be a pro-active way to deal with long term relationships, which friends of mine did years ago. Both having been married before, and both having parented children, they decided when they married that they would go out for dinner once a month and renew their vows. They did this until he eventually died.

I thought this was an incredibly creative way to keep saying *yes* to one another!

5. EMOTIONALLY HEALTHY PEOPLE WANT AND CAN APPRECIATE A DEEP CONNECTION WITH EACH OTHER

6. EMOTIONALLY HEALTHY PEOPLE KNOW HOW TO BE PRESENT

I have written about this ability in the next chapter on Being Present.

7. EMOTIONALLY HEALTHY PEOPLE CAN SEE CLEARLY

They see phenomenologically, in detail, as if they were writing a novel about this character sitting in front of them. They don't rush to conclusions as to what meaning they make of what they see. They just see the other, are present with that person, without generalizing or judging.

8. EMOTIONALLY HEALTHY PEOPLE CAN HEAR LITERALLY

Hearing literally many can't do. Often we hear our interpretation of what one is saying. If there is a discrepancy between someone's tone of voice and the words, such as in "Of course I love you!", the other can hear this and ask for a more congruent statement, which is easier said than done in many instances, especially if you are a young child.

9. EMOTIONALLY HEALTHY PEOPLE TAKE GOOD CARE OF THEMSELVES AND THEIR LOVED ONES

Be careful of one member being the caretaker in all situations, which means he or she might not take the time to care for him or her self. Both need a little caretaking now and then. And beware that caretaking can become spoiling the other...!

10. EMOTIONALLY HEALTHY PEOPLE CAN CREATE EGALITARIAN STRUCTURES WHEREVER IT IS APPROPRIATE IN THEIR RELATIONSHIPS AND COMMUNITIES

- They make joint decisions
- They support one another's creativity and interests
- They seek win-win ways for everyone in their families and communities.

11. EMOTIONALLY HEALTHY PEOPLE SHARE A LOT OF VALUES

- Good will
- Caring
- Respect
- Aliveness
- Awareness of self and other

- Flexibility
- Openness to the unexpected
- Willingness to take risks
- Celebrate other people
- Aren't afraid to ask for help
- Get their happiness and satisfaction within.
  "You're never as good or as bad as people say you are."
- Speak with certainty
- Rarely pass judgment
- Congruent: in alignment with their higher selves
- Take responsibility for self and actions
- Willingness to look at themselves deeply
- Compassion for self and others

12. EMOTIONALLY HEALTHY PEOPLE CAN ACKNOWLEDGE MISTAKES

Healthy couples are willing to acknowledge mistakes when they make them. They understand that blaming is not useful, so they take the blame when it is due them, and expect others to acknowledge blame when it is due them. They are open to feedback from their partners and can give useful feedback to others if asked. They are open to seeking professional help if they think they could benefit from it.

13. THOM HARTMANN: ON SUCCESSFUL RELATIONSHIPS

Caring couples show interest and curiosity in their partner's interests, even if they don't share them.

If one says: "Look at that gorgeous bird." The other, who is not into birds, says: "I see it. I know you are thrilled with seeing this bird, and he is impressive."

So maximize this idea and see what you come up with... being interested or showing interest in... what makes your partner happy or excited.

"I'm fully present in the
Here & Now with you!"

2. Being Present

"Compassion is not a relationship between the healer and the wounded. It is a relationship between equals. Only when we know our own darkness well can be present with the darkness of others. Compassion becomes real when we recognize our shared humanity."

– Pema Chödrön

These words are becoming more and more known, and more and more people are learning how to be present with one another. Gestalt Institutes and Centers teach their students how to do this, Mindfulness programs teach this, and many others are reading about this and practicing this as well.

A few years ago a colleague of mine was writing up his therapy notes for his supervisor. He had not been trained in Gestalt therapy, and thought he was following the regulation to describe the person he interviewed without being judgmental. He wrote:

"A 25-year-old very attractive woman came in for therapy today, complaining of..."

This is *NOT* a non-judgmental comment! The observer is judging this woman to be "very attractive." If the observer is feeling attracted to her, he or she is noticing his own self awareness, and this is different than labeling her as an attractive woman. Many of us confuse our judgments, which can be positive as well as negative, with our phenomenological descriptions of what we experience.

But back to being present. Two people who are learning how to be present with one another such as a couple or a two students, may wish to share their full awareness of being with the other, including any emotional or sexual attraction. And their awareness may also include noticing how the other speaks, their postures and gestures, the words they use, what they hear and don't hear, and so on.

Developing this very specific kind of awareness and attention is rare for many people, particularly during these recent times when everyone is so preoccupied with their smart phones and laptops. Many people don't know how to be present with one another which can affect relationships a lot.

People want to be seen, heard and understood, unless they have something to hide, which some do. So when someone is really present, many are shocked, as they've never had this kind of attention before. And usually people like it.

But it requires learning how to hear and see more clearly and accurately. As I've mentioned before many of us see in concepts: "I see an attractive woman" or "I see a skinny sickly child." There may be no agreement that others would see this woman as attractive, or this child as sickly and skinny. Again these are concepts, judgments, and not phenomenological observations.

Others often hear their interpretations of what someone is saying, and do not hear what they literally are saying.

> *"You said you were unhappy because your parents didn't like Chicago."*

> *"No, I didn't say that. I said I was unhappy because my parents didn't like working in Chicago. I wish you would listen to me more closely!"*

This isn't our fault, but the difficulty with our language and culture more than anything. English is often vague. We often say things inaccurately

EXPERIMENT
Sit comfortably close to the person you wish to be present with; listen to them literally, and be sure you are observing them accurately, without judging.

3.   Dealing Well With Conflict

We all know that conflict is the number one issue most people are concerned with and have little ability to deal with. Hopefully some of these ideas will be helpful to you and your partner.

For starters, everyone has conflict at some point, whether expressed or not. If it isn't expressed, intuitive and aware people pick up that something isn't in order, and react or try to clarify what is going on between them.

Recently a social support group of mostly Gestalt oriented friends and colleagues met. One member was hurt by something another member did and told her in the group setting. She responded with regret for having hurt him without realizing it. He unfortunately began labeling her, which she didn't respond to at the time. She sat with it following the meeting and vowed to share this with him at the next gathering a couple of months away.

- He described quite accurately what she said to him that hurt him.
- And shared how that made him feel.
- She respected his ability to clearly report the incident, which fit with her memory of it. And she respected how that could have made him feel.
- But his assumptions were wrong about what was going on with her, and there was no way he could have known this without her sharing it, which she did. And what was going on with her had nothing to do with him.

I SEE, I THINK, I FEEL

Back in the 1970s when family therapy training was an important ability for psychotherapists in the Bay Area, we were taught a helpful and simple process:

1. What did you see or hear about your partner (I SEE)

2. What did this make you think (I THINK)

3. How did all of this then make you feel (I FEEL)

This easy-to-understand process has helped many of my clients in their interactions with one another. It is all about the one who brings up the issue, at least in the beginning.

SEE: I *saw* you looking down when I told you about what happened to me yesterday.

THINK: And that made me *think* you didn't care about me or my mother.

FEEL: And then I *felt* hurt.

So in this example the woman told the man what she said that made him interpret her behavior as uncaring, which then led to his feeling hurt.

The idea is not to see conflict as winning or losing. Instead it opens a way for two people to learn to listen to one another and perhaps understand some things about that person they didn't know or understand before.

Since it is election time now in the USA, let's imagine a couple: one is for Bernie Sanders, the other for Hillary Clinton. When these two get going, sparks start to fly as each criticizes the other for one reason or another. It is easy to leave things like that and to agree to disagree, as some like to say. However, we can go further with this analogy by asking some questions.

- Has either been *curious* as to why their partner supports one over the other?
- Are you open to hearing the answer to this from your partner?
- Often we just attack and don't ask: "How did you arrive at the conclusion that you wanted to support Hillary, or Bernie?"
- Maybe we'd learn something about ourselves if we were open to learning such from our partners or friends or colleagues.
- Give it a try the next time someone is critical of you for your election preference.

I **see**, I **think**, and I **feel** as a reminder of when things go awry with someone you love. Teach this to him or her as well, so that you both can benefit from this idea.

BRAINSTORMING

Many people like this way of working with conflict. Let's say you and your partner have a conflict over where to go on vacation this next summer.

1. Get a pack of 3x5 index cards

2. Spread them around a table

3. Put one idea on a card

4. Keep on going until you both feel finished

5. Don't evaluate any items until all are on the table

6. Organize cards into topics and categories

7. Keep on being creative as you look for a solution to your conflict!

8. Devise ways to compromise, negotiate, and agree to disagree plus all the implications of that with each issue

    a. Create a space for time to explain your *understanding* and feelings to your partner.
    b. Those who dislike this approach, which can lead to long explanations and discussions, could create a system of giving one another short clear messages that are non-judgmental yet do the job:
    Ouch
    My Turn
    Thank you
    Oops, sorry

EXPLANATIONS

We are often prone to wanting to explain ourselves once we are accused of something. It seems that this is human nature. It probably is, but we all know how un-useful it often is, as seldom do our explanations settle a conflict! And the time it takes to hear each other out, could be endless.

Here are a couple of examples of responses to explanations.

One couple I worked with years ago, didn't like the long explanations, and this seemed to anger one of them especially. So they found a way to let each other know whenever the other one did something that felt hurtful to the other... and they did this by simply saying "ouch". This helped them a lot, and they didn't need to go into long explanations with one another. They got the message quickly and easily!

* * *

Another couple I knew had a drum set at one end of their living room, and another set at the other end of the room. When they were angry with one another, they went after each other on the drums. This approach worked very well for them.

OUTSIDE HELP

Once you have tried a number of different ways to work through things, or to find a solution to different issues between the two of you, perhaps you might like to hire a couples therapist or a mediator to work with the two of you. Not only might this help resolve whatever your issue is with one another, but it might help in bringing to your awareness things you hadn't considered about yourself and about your partner.

In the above example at the gathering, the person who was accused of doing something that the other felt hurt by, suddenly became tearful as she realized a few things about herself that she had been burdened with for some time. These were not in her awareness at the time, but afterwards she felt much clearer about the difficult times she'd been having lately.

Most common reasons causing conflict that I've found in my practice with couples are:

- Feeling misunderstood
- Feeling discounted, dismissed

These are both signs of not experiencing the other fully or not taking the time to be fully present with your partner.

RESOURCES

Maybe you and your partner can find something easy like this to try. Be creative! Two books that we used that were helpful to couples and partners are:

- *Intimate Enemy*, Richard Bach
- *Do I Have To Give Up Me To Be Loved By You*? Jordan and Margaret Paul

4.　Curiosity

This is one of my favorite themes. It is my contention that often couples don't know as much about one another as they might like, and for some reason they don't allow themselves to be curious. They give lots of reasons for not asking their partners things they'd like to know.

My favorite is: "She'd tell me if she wanted me to know." This might be true, but also she is capable of taking care of herself, and if she doesn't want to answer a question of yours, she'll say no to you. So this could just be another way to avoid being told NO. (See chapter on Being Direct: Hearing and Saying NO.)

Often, when working with couples who have been together for a long time, I will suggest they go out on a date, say to a nice dinner, and during that time together they indulge their curiosity. Tell each other something about yourself the other doesn't know. This may not be the best setting to tell your spouse you slept with someone else, but you will discover many things you haven't shared, I'm sure.

Many of us probably had our curiosity dampened, when at two and a half, we were motor-mouths asking a zillion questions beginning with "why?" Don't let this experience stop you from asking questions as an adult!

Remember most of us want to be seen and known for who we really are.

As Erv Polster's book, *Everyone's Life Is Worth A Novel*, supports the importance and interesting-ness of each of us. We all have an inner novel. In fact, you might be so curious that you will help him or her write it for posterity! It is worth it. And be sure to add some photos as well.

For some years I've worked part time in nursing homes in the Pacific Northwest. On a few occasions I've invited clients to tell me their life stories, which with the help of their family members, turned into mini autobiographies for them to give to their family and friends. Just helping them recall was an enormous delight for most of them, as they regained a lost sense of self. One person whose autobiography I did was a Vietnam Veteran. Another was the daughter of a Hollywood stage director, whose family friends were well-known actors and actresses.

I think my curiosity about others is what led me to become a therapist. I recall years ago, before I got my degree, I wanted to work in the international relations field somehow. I gave up this desire when I couldn't find the right job in New York City in my early 20s. However, I always retained my insatiable curiosity about others and their lives. So I became a psychotherapist, which gave me permission to ask people a lot of questions I might not have given myself permission to ask otherwise!

NOT BEING OPEN TO OTHER PERSON'S POINT OF VIEW

Usually when someone disagrees with us, we go on the defensive and begin to think of ways to make our case and to convince the *other* of our position. This stance is regrettable, as usually we don't fully hear the disagreement. How rare it is to show interest or curiosity in the other person's opinion!

Just watch typical debates. Usually the other person has crafted a response in anticipation of being disagreed with, so there is no real sharing or dialogue. There is no curiosity, no interest in learning something new. Debates are ways to play the game of *gotcha*, or *I win–you lose*, rather than opportunities to learn from one another. They are shams, as we can see watching the USA political 'debates'.

EXPERIMENT

1. *Swallow your ego (easier said than done), and become genuinely curious.*

2. *Then allow yourself to be curious about your partner's point of view.*

Good luck and enjoy, even if you don't agree!

Section F

Important Themes

1. Success / Failure Paradigm

2. Our Inner Authoritarian Conflict

3. Togetherist / Separatist Dynamics

4. Contact Withdrawal Dynamic

1.   Success / Failure Paradigm

It seems very common these days for people to constantly evaluate whether they are a success or a failure at whatever they do, say, or experience. It becomes like a mantra to the many inner critics or Topdogs that evaluate their every move. They are often relentless!

Just take the normal American greeting: "How are you?" Note how you respond to this question. Most people 'go into their heads' and ask themselves how they are, and then attempt to answer this question by evaluating whether they are doing things successfully or not, and then deciding if, in answering, they will tell their truth or not... if they chose to answer the question at all!

If a person is very watchful of this inner evaluation process, it could keep them away and distracted—they are so busy evaluating their 'self' that it cuts into any experience they might be having right now, such as taking a walk, making love, taking in the nature around them.

THE MEASURING SCALE

More importantly however, is that this imaginary scale we hold in our heads to evaluate ourselves, may be flawed from the beginning. It may fit in school, learning academic subjects, but is it good to use everywhere and all the time, including about our relationships?

DO YOU WANT TO LIVE BY THIS PARADIGM?

We've been raised on this paradigm in school and probably from our parents as well. In school we are given grades, and constantly being compared to our fellow students. "He got an A and I only got a C+", "She is better than I am." She becomes depressed, and may end up in the therapist's office.

In Gestalt classes we call this dynamic an *introjection*, which we accepted from our family or community. We have the choice of whether we want to continue to accept it or not, or how big a role we want it to have in our lives.

I personally do not think it is applicable to relationships. When people say they failed at marriage because they got a divorce, I cringe. I don't think anyone fails at relationships. Our partners are important connections in our lives that may bring up a lot of our issues, and hopefully we will be able to work through them, whether we stay together or not.

Success and failure are not a part of this experience in my book. If it were, I'd be discussing a lot of ideas to bring you success. They would probably be taken by you as *shoulds,* and then you would have something else to criticize yourself for if you didn't learn these lessons accurately.

These ideas are for you to experiment with, to find what fits and works for you, not in a manipulative way, but in a genuine way.

They are not skills, but awarenesses. They *shouldn't*, pardon my use of this word, be used to try to manipulate or try to change others.

> *Recently someone said they wanted more skills to be able to reach a family member. I realized it was for the purpose of trying to change that person, rather than just be with that person without an agenda. Luckily she was able to put her agenda aside, and they had better contact than they had had in a long time.*

She let go of the agenda she had for her family member, and got away from evaluating herself and her sister in a success/failure way, and became present with her. What emerged in their relationship was something a lot more genuine and caring, which thrilled them both.

So do watch if and when this paradigm is running your life. I think you will be a lot more peaceful and happier if you aren't so subservient to it. Remember it is an introjection, and not necessarily something you decided to give such a prominent role to in your life.

Inner Authoritarian Conflict

2.   Our Inner Authoritarian Conflict: Meet Topdog and Underdog

Up until this chapter we've been exploring many aspects of egalitarian relationships with a partner. Now it is time to look at the relationship inside ourselves: that voice inside our head that loves to criticize us, and the other one that may respond. Gestalt therapists refer to these warring parts of ourselves as Topdog and Underdog.

TOPDOG

Topdog's mission is to make us the person we think we want to be in this world. Unfortunately he tries to keep us in line by being authoritarian, by telling us what we should or should not do, by giving us advice, by yelling at us, putting us down, ridiculing and discounting us. Some people have said their Topdog is good for them, that they need this reminding voice. And these same people report how one of their parents took this role with them as they needed it. Others feel the opposite, they don't need or want any part of themselves telling them what to do, feel and think all the time.

> *"You should be ashamed by what you did, teasing your little brother like that.. You are a bully, just like your father said you are."*
>
> * * *
>
> *"You got another C in History? You aren't going to amount to anything with those kinds of grades. You are destined to be a failure, just like your Uncle Pete."*
>
> * * *
>
> *I remember years ago observing two small children under five playing house during a family therapy session. One was clearly imitating one of her parents as she shook her finger at the other child and yelled orders at him. And told her if she didn't behave she was going to punish him, to spank him very hard. We develop Topdogs at an early age and they can be around forever!"*

SUCCESS / FAILURE PARADIGM—TOPDOG'S FAVORITE

Often Topdogs are caught up in the paradigm of Success/Failure, such a common paradigm in our USA culture. This orientation pushes us to evaluate every waking moment to see if we are doing all we can to be successful! It encourages us to make judgments constantly as well from where we are to where we think we want to be on the success ladder! It is overwhelming to me just writing about this dynamic in our lives. It is at the root of so much self loathing and keeps our Topdogs extremely busy. The areas it likes to delve into are numerous.

- Are you successful in your career?
- Are you successful financially?
- Are you successfully healthy?
- Are you successful at keeping yourself attractive and fit?
- Are you successful at being a good person?
- Are you successful at being in a marriage or relationship?
- Are you successful as a parent?

As our culture changes, hopefully, from a success/failure paradigm to a good-enough paradigm, our Topdogs may relax a little.

UNDERDOG

The part of us that might respond is Underdog. Some folks aren't aware of having such a character inside themselves. Underdog may be in hiding, both from ourselves as well as from others. So what that part of us is up to we may not know. Our Underdog may comply with Topdog, ignore him, try to manipulate him, or come out of hiding and directly confront him about the authoritarian way he is treating us. Or in some cases we might get depressed and say to ourselves that Topdog is right.

Even if Topdog has a point about the content of the remarks: "You were being very mean to your brother yesterday," Underdog may be responding to Topdog yelling at him while wagging his finger at him. The process is very authoritarian, leading usually to an anxious and depressed inner life. Most of us don't like to be treated this way by others, and here we are treating ourselves this way, just like our parents may have done.

Here are some examples of Underdog.

> *"You are right. I am a worthless slob. I'll try to do better next time."*

> *"I didn't mean to sound that way. I'm sorry. I must be a bad person."*

> *"All you ever do is tell me what to do. You have no compassion or understanding, and I'm sick of you. Get out of my life. I don't need you to keep me in line anymore. I'm doing just fine without you."*

The worst part about these voices is they often talk *at* us incessantly, and often keep us awake at night. Over and over again Topdog goes after us. She can make us anxious, convince us we are worthless, and lead us into depression. She can distract us whenever and wherever she wants. If we are doing something we enjoy, she may give us a hard time. If we are with someone we love, she may distract us so much that we cannot be very present with our partner if she is constantly yelling at us!

Eventually some will go into therapy to deal with these inner tortuous voices. It isn't easy to get rid of Topdog, so don't have too high expectations!

> *Jim Simkin, PhD, (colleague of Fritz Perls, MD, co-founder of Gestalt Therapy), taught Gestalt therapy at his home in Big Sur, California, and often told his students that he (his Underdog) had tried to get rid of his Topdog for years. As his Underdog he refused to listen to Topdog, got furious with him, agreed with him, ignored him, put him down. None of these strategies worked. His Topdog kept on bullying him, day in and day out. Finally Jim decided to let him be, to accept him, but not to take him to heart. Instead every time his Topdog appeared, Jim would wave to him, let him have his say, and move on. "I stopped **indulging** him, and even though he kept coming back, I wasn't so bothered by him anymore. I couldn't change him, so I just let him be." And Jim reported he became more peaceful after that.*

So what Jim did to become more peaceful, was to have a dialogue with these two parts of himself. He did this more than once, perhaps many times. He'd have his Topdog in one chair, and his Underdog in another, and he'd role play each by switching chairs back and forth, disagreeing, explaining, laughing, crying, yelling, feeling guilty, feeling ashamed, learning more from one another about their different points of view. Over time, this kind of role playing can lead to a new synthesis, and new understanding, which happened in his case. Jim accepted him, and didn't indulge him. And he still had to put up with his Topdog!

Our internal Topdogs and Underdogs are not alike; their personalities are usually different, and some Topdogs are more vicious than others. Some try to be understanding, but are still authoritarian.

Other ways to deal with these voices, is to write a dialogue between them, or draw or paint this dynamic… any way that helps us understand one another better, just like they are a couple inside us.

HOW OUR INNER AUTHORITARIAN CONFLICT AND EGALITARIAN RELATIONSHIPS INTERFACE

The theme of this book is about egalitarian relationships, and I am wondering if we have an authoritarian relationship inside of us that natters at us incessantly, is it possible to have an egalitarian relationship with another person in real life? I don't know the answer to this, but I am hypothesizing that it could make things more difficult for us. If I am treating myself with disdain and criticism, perhaps I'll do the same to my partner, or expect my partner to treat me this way.

So as you read this book, and experiment with broadening your egalitarian ways with your loved ones, see if your inner critic is getting in your way. You might want to get some help to neutralize your Topdog, or get him to treat you as an equal, if possible. Hopefully this book will help you learn how to do that on all levels, inside and out!

EXPERIMENTS

1. *Get clear about the tone of voice and the kinds of things your Topdog says to your Underdog.*

2. *Role play them talking to one another.*

3. *Write their script.*

4. *Have them keep in dialogue for a long time, hopefully until they come to a new understanding.*

5. *Check out the pressure your Topdog puts on you to be successful in all of the categories above.*

6. *See what it is like to change those statements to "good-enough." Do you feel any different when you do this?*

7. *Since we all have blind spots, a Gestalt therapist or friend might be helpful to have with you when you do this.*

Togetherist / Separatist Dynamic

"I need to be with you!"

"I need alone time!"

3. Togetherist / Separatist Dynamics

ENMESHMENT

"He felt now that he was not simply close to her, but that he did not know where he ended and she began."

– Leo Tolstoy, *Anna Karenina*

After having taught family therapy and Gestalt therapy for many years, I began connecting a lot of dots in working with people in relationships, including my own. I devised this working model based on what I observed in many of my students' and clients' partnerships and marriages.

So now let's look more specifically at this model from my point of view. In it are two main characters, that I've over-generalized about for the purpose of clarity. Each of you readers may identify with one more than the other at this time in your life, and these generalizations may not fit you exactly. Hopefully however, this model will be as useful to you as it has been to many over the years.

THE TOGETHERIST

This person reaches out to be in contact with the other. It is part of her persona. She doesn't feel like a whole person unless with a partner, fears abandonment and is afraid of being isolated and alone.

THE SEPARATIST

This person is someone who needs to be alone more than the Togetherist to feel like a whole person. He fears losing himself in the other, becoming enmeshed, and is afraid of being smothered.

THE SEPARATIST AND THE TOGETHERIST
Symbol: **//**

Two lines on an angle. This represents the Togetherist reaching for the Separatist, as the Separatist walks in the other direction. Both are leaning at an angle and neither is standing on their own two feet. The more the Togetherist reaches, the more the Separatist pulls away. They stay the same distance from one another, rarely able to come into full contact with one another. Both feel dissatisfied, particularly the Togetherist, who may seek therapy to get the Separatist to change.

TWO SEPARATISTS
Symbol: **\ /**

Again neither is standing on their own two feet. They lean away from one another. They live together with little contact, each doing his own thing. Neither wants much from the other, at least for awhile. If one realizes he wants closer contact with the other, this system begins to break down.

TWO TOGETHERISTS
Symbol: **/**

Again neither is standing on their own two feet. They lean towards each other, totally enmeshed. They may feel like "It's you and me against the world, Baby", and often they keep others outside of their cocoon. Everything is fine for awhile. Then one may realize she is missing a lot and begins spending more time outside their duo. This may cause the system to falter and eventually break down.

A WELL BALANCED PERSON AND A TOGETHERIST
Symbol: **| **

If a well balanced person, who can stand on his own two feet comfortably, is in a relationship with a Togetherist, the well balanced one may begin to "look like" a Separatist after awhile. The Togetherist will probably be wanting more of his time than he would like to give, so he may seek therapy or leave the relationship to find a healthier mate.

A WELL BALANCED PERSON AND A SEPARATIST
Symbol: | /

The same is true of the well balanced person in relationship with a Separatist. She will begin to "look like" a Togetherist after awhile, as her need for normal contact is not getting met. She may find seeing her partner so infrequently becomes intolerable to her, and she either may seek help or leave the relationship for a healthier mate.

TWO HEALTHY WELL BALANCED PEOPLE
Symbol: ||

Ideally these two people in relationship are standing on their own two feet, not leaning, as all of the others are, except occasionally when one is stressed, sick or in need of support from the other. But not as a general rule. They have a good balance between contact and withdrawal (see Contact Withdrawal chapter), and are minimally afraid of enmeshment or abandonment. From this place, they can make deep contact with one another and enjoy their separateness. On occasion when under stress one might be a little more needy than usual, or need more alone time than usual. Hopefully, a couple can discuss these aspects about themselves.

* * *

Over the years I've asked many students and clients about their experiences of this model. Many identify being in the same role in a number of relationships. Others find they experience both, within a relationship and over time with different partners.

I also asked them which role they prefer! Here is a summary of their responses:

- The ones who chose the Togetherist said they would rather experience being abandoned, being humiliated and hurt by someone they love, rather than have to deal with the guilt of rejecting their partner.

- The ones who chose the Separatist preferred to reject someone and feel guilty rather than have to deal with feelings of humiliation and abandonment. Feeling enmeshed was intolerable to these folks.

The Togetherist may go into therapy as he keeps feeling abandoned and wonders what is wrong with him. The Separatist probably feels therapy is unnecessary.

Now as I rewrite this 30 years later, I realize that in this model I've used images of people that are quite one sided and restricted. If you were to draw a continuum line with Separatist at one end and Togetherist at the other end, there would be many places along this line where we might put ourselves, and different places with different people. So please keep this in mind as you explore this model in your own life.

Demonstrating the Gestalt concept of Contact/Withdrawal in this way, helps students and clients "get it." And I often have them role play this dynamic with others in the class or couples' system, often in silence using body language only and no words. Back and forth, connecting and disconnecting, from moment to moment in the here and now.

FEARS

Let's look at the fears: abandonment and engulfment—two sides of the same coin? Perhaps. Each person privy to this model can see how many people fall into each of these states if their contact isn't satisfying. The Togetherist may try to manipulate or convince the Separatist to be more contactful. The Separatist may try to manipulate or convince the Togetherist to enjoy more separation.

And sometimes Togetherist therapists may push for more contact between couples without fully exploring their own issues, and seeing the subtle nuances which the client may have difficulty clarifying in words.

And sometimes the Separatist therapist might support more private alone time with his Separatist clients without being aware of the subtle nuances of this stance, and what he or she might be missing with couples.

EXPERIMENTS FOR COUPLES

1. *Talk to one another about which role you each tend to play. And you may share memories of why it is this way with you. If you felt abandoned when young, for example, this probably left a strong mark on you. Or if you experienced being smothered, this also might*

have left a strong mark on you. Being open and vulnerable about these early experiences can be healing in itself for both parties.

2. *Role playing each other can be very helpful if the couple is open and not too threatened by this suggestion. It is important to see this as an experiment, not as a 'should'. You can do this in silence, only using body language, or using words with your role play as well.*

3. *And if you decide to change your behavior, remember it takes time, and no one can be expected to change over night.*

4. *The more you work on this, the more likely the Togetherist can tolerate more space between moments of contact, and the Separatist can tolerate more closeness without losing himself.*

SYNCHRONICITY

After I had put these ideas together back in the late 1970s and had been teaching them at the original Gestalt Institute of San Francisco for awhile, I discovered that others had also devised similar models around the same time, unbeknownst to me. A Gestalt therapist in Southern California had devised a similar model, and a book came out, a cartoon book actually, which showed a similar dynamic. At the time many of my colleagues were astonished at the synchronicity of these three events. Some of my colleagues and I wondered if this was an example of the 100th Monkey phenomenon.[1]

And this could lead into a whole other exploratory avenue of where our ideas come from, the role of universal energies in our thinking, and other such questions. But this isn't the main theme of this book, so I won't address these ideas now.

---

1   From Wikipedia: The hundredth monkey effect is a purported phenomenon in which a new behavior or idea is claimed to spread rapidly by unexplained means from one group to all related groups once a critical number of members of one group exhibit the new behavior or acknowledge the new idea.[1] The account of such a phenomenon originated with Lawrence Blair and Lyall Watson in the mid-to-late 1970s, who claimed that it was the observation of Japanese scientists.

4. Contact Withdrawal Dynamic

This dynamic, which is a key teaching point in Gestalt Therapy, has been a wonderful help to many couples I've worked with over the years.

It has to do with discovering our natural rhythm of contact and withdrawal, which we all have. After all, we are awake and make contact with whomever we need to during the day and at night we sleep, hopefully, withdrawing from the world for a certain amount of time. This is one obvious rhythm for the two of them. Many others exist as well. How long can I work doing my job before I need a break. How long do you need. Can we meet in between when we are both rested and relaxed. Or does one of us have to give up some of our alone time or together time to accommodate the other.

Couples are forever crying about how often they spend time together; one is forever too busy to spend as much time as the first wishes, and the other one has too much time for his partner, so complaints go. (See Separatist/Togetherist Chapter.)

ORGANISMIC SELF REGULATION

Look at an infant now in your mind's eye. He has to learn to follow the rhythm of his parents, regarding when to eat and sleep, and when to be awake and in contact with them and others. Often his parents' schedules don't work for the growing child, but he adapts anyway. Then the school system comes in with its schedule, and maybe the religious organizations, the sports teams, and so on. As the child grows up he may have no idea what his "natural rhythm" of contact and withdrawal is, so he just does the best he can to keep up with the demands of his family and community. And then doctors and other specialists inform us that we need X hours of sleep, completely oblivious to our individual needs.

So sometimes in psychotherapy sessions, my clients begin to attune to what their rhythms are, and begin to honor them as best they can given their jobs and other duties of living.

There have been many a class or group of mine to which someone has arrived with not enough sleep. Since most of my classes were scheduled in a room full of pillows, I would encourage people to take care of themselves, and if they needed to sleep or nod off, to do so. I just didn't want them to leave the room. This honored many who were off center from not enough sleep the night before.

Finding our own rhythm can include not only our daily schedules, but vacations as well. Some may need to do something very energetic on vacation; the other may need to relax and slow down in their lives. The other person may ideally require a beach setting for a vacation. Then they might have quite a time creating a vacation that works for both of them.... Or they could plan one for him, another for her, and time in between for them both.

Friendships and having guests over is another issue that comes up in this context. Do we let friends drop in? Or do we prefer they call first? Many troubles come up around these issues, again one of contact/withdrawal rhythms of the couple.

> *Not long ago a client wanted some help about what to do with his in-laws coming over whenever they felt like it. His partner had even given his own family a key! In working with them on this issue, they realized this should be a joint issue, since it was "their" house. The in-laws were reluctant to give up their key, but they eventually got the point.*

I'm sure you get the picture. It is interesting that now in parts of Washington State the school system is changing its schedule for high school kids to come later to school in the mornings, to try to adjust to their rhythms more accurately. This could be a huge change nationwide!

So once couples have a sense of one another's rhythms as well as their own, then they may need to tweak their egalitarian structure to accommodate these rhythms more accurately.

The important thing is to know what our ideal rhythm is, and to honor it as much as possible, being creative about a couple's time together. Also, our rhythms change as we age, and some don't have the stamina they had when they were young. Keep remembering the only constant in life is change.

PSYCHOLOGICAL IMPLICATIONS OF THIS

As you know or can easily imagine, people can feel abandoned or enmeshed if they perceive their partner either is demanding too much of their time, or not enough of it. Attending to these issues is of prime importance not only to the client's understanding of their natural rhythm of contact and withdrawal, but of deep seated unresolved issues which may get provoked by being together too little or too much, depending on your perception.

For example, if two Togetherists are a couple, there will probably be a tight bond between them, and difficulty if either of them develops a friendship with someone outside their tight system. Often this dynamic is referred to as "It's me and you against the world, Baby."

> *Years ago a Gestalt student of mine was in a marriage for 25 years that she described as their being very enmeshed with one another. Her being in training was a huge threat to her husband. She was relieved and astounded to see how their super togetherness was not necessarily the "perfect" love, but rather a huge protection from a system she didn't particularly agree with. I don't know what happened to them after she finished training, but I know she was on the road of expanding her circle of acquaintances and friends.*

This particular dynamic is often present in relationships where there is an authoritarian male together with a submissive female. He basically owns her, she feels. This has been a model for many, many generations… unfortunately, and has nothing to do with egalitarian relationships!

Section G

Unhealthy Dynamics

1. **Experiments Versus Shoulds!**

2. **Interpretations and Misinterpretations**

3. **Ping-Pong**

4. **Unsolicited Advice**

5. **Yes / But**

6. **'We' Versus 'I'**

7. **Manipulation**

8. **Speaking Dysfunctions**

9. **The Hit and Run Dynamic**

10. **Discounting: Verbal and Non-Verbal**

11. **Talking *At* Rather Than *To* The Other Person**

12. **Admitting Mistakes**

13. **Truth Telling**

14. **Lead Lines**

15. **Giving-In To Avoid Conflict**

16. **Just**

17. **You Need To Change, So I Will Feel Better**

18. **We *Should* Talk This Over Now!**

19. **Silences**

20. **I Can't Trust You Anymore**

21. **Expectations and Assumptions Versus Hopes and Desires**

1.   Experiments Versus Shoulds!

This section will be filled with many of the common foibles which cause couples to turn off of one another. When people identify with one of the games they play or behaviors that drives their partner nuts, their immediate response is to set up a *new should* for themselves.

As a Gestalt therapist who subscribes to people finding what ways suit them best, I encourage everyone reading this section to try on new behaviors as **Experiments, and stay away from giving yourself some new rules or shoulds.**

An experiment can help you check out what works best for you and your partner. It is an opportunity to try something new, which can be an adventure… rather than setting up a new rule without having experimented first.

For example: if your partner has a tendency to tell long stories without finding out if you have time right now to listen, **experiment** with asking her to give you a lead line or a paragraph heading. Don't make it a *should*, or you will just make matters worse.

Learning new behaviors isn't easy. Even if we are psychologically fine with the new behavior, it takes time to make the new behavior a habit. Be gentle with yourself and your partner! Don't expect each of you to change overnight.

Another way of exploring these new behaviors, is to follow the Digestive Model that Fritz Perls was inclined to use. For example, he would encourage us to taste a new behavior, try it on, see if we like the taste. And if we don't, throw it up, and try another one that suits us better. Often when we feel *disgust* for something, we feel sick and want to get rid of it. If you don't, it might give you a stomach ache.

Remember ***new shoulds*** become more ammunition for one to attack the other, defeating the whole purpose of learning some new healthier ways to relate.

2.   Interpretations and Misinterpretations

A most common foible, is our skill at making interpretations of what others are thinking and feeling or why they behave in some particular way. We humans want to understand things, and if the reasons aren't obvious we make them up. Let's look at this a little more closely.

> *Susie falls and hits her head on the sidewalk. Being an avid drinker, her partner immediately interprets this event as being a result of too much alcohol. She is judged severely by her partner and ignored for awhile. Eventually someone helps her to the medical clinic where she was diagnosed as having had a stroke.*

The partner did not take the time to get close enough to her to *see* if she had any symptoms of alcoholism, or other possibilities such as stroke or heart attack. *He interpreted the data incorrectly. He made an assumption that wasn't true.*

Often these misinterpretations happen because we don't know how or what data to gather. Often we are in a hurry and won't slow down unless it is obvious that it is a serious matter. In this case it was important to keep an *open mind* until the doctors could gather their data.

We often assume our first thought or intuition is correct. This is almost like taking on the role of judge and jury before all the evidence has been presented. We wouldn't allow this in a court of law. And in this age of speed and forgetfulness, people don't slow down enough to see accurately, hear clearly, and use their other senses as well, before pronouncing judgment.

Are you aware of having made a misinterpretation in the past? Most of us have at some point in our lives, and probably many times.

EXPERIMENTS

See if you can recall any times when you misinterpreted what was going on with your partner and yourself.

1. *Does this happen very often? If so, it is possible that you don't listen carefully or see accurately?*

2. *Slow down and gather more information and facts.*

3. *Bring others into the mix, such as the doctor in the above case.*

4. *Invite an open dialogue where each can express their feelings towards one another about this incident and others, if relevant.*

5. *If you get "stuck" seek help from a professional Gestalt couples therapist, if there is one in your community.*

3. Ping-Pong

This common dynamic I call Ping-Pong. Here is how it is played.

He says, "You promised to go with me to the jazz club tonight and now you are reneging on me, just because you don't feel like it. I am upset and angry, as I thought we had an agreement."

She says, not responding to his comment, "Well, two weeks ago you reneged on me when we were going to go to my parents for dinner." (Implication: since you did the same thing you have no right to call me out on it!)

She experiences him as blaming her; she blames back. They are at a stalemate and neither situation gets worked through or understood.

Instead of completing the interaction he started above, she changes the subject and brings up something he did that upset her, as a way of deflecting and protecting herself.

Usually neither interaction gets completed when one does this. They are at an uncomfortable stalemate, and she has convinced him he doesn't have a right to complain, since he did the same thing.

EXPERIMENTS
Can you think of many times when you and your partner played ping-pong?

1. *How did you feel after the incomplete interactions and blaming?*
2. *Become aware of when you both do this.*
3. *Discuss it.*
4. *Perhaps even role play it on purpose, exaggerating the dynamic to make you super clear of how it works!*
5. *Then when it happens, one of the couple can suggest completing interaction A before going to interaction B.*

4.   Unsolicited Advice

"*Stop trying to control your life (and your partner's), it gets in the way of Divine Intervention.*"

– author unknown

In many relationships one takes on the role of the helper or the rescuer. This person is constantly trying to fix or help the other. Usually this role makes the helper feel useful. However, often the recipient doesn't ask for this help, or advice, and feels demeaned by it always being offered by her partner. She feels one-down, and may eventually resent his seeming superiority. Often this dynamic allows the helper to never be vulnerable, and to always feel more together than her partner. Helpers often become teachers and therapists and avoid having to face or discuss their own issues and problems.

Peter was cooking breakfast one Sunday. Robert came into the kitchen on the run, telling Peter he was not cooking the eggs quite right, and he would show him how to do this. Robert loved being helpful. Peter did not love Robert's helpfulness, and told him to get out of the kitchen and let him do the cooking his way. Robert, thinking he was the good guy, couldn't understand why Peter didn't see things the same way he did! So, they were off and running with being hurt and angry with one another.

* * *

As in the title of this book, Don't Tell Me What To Do... Ask Me!, *Peter would have preferred that Robert ask him if he wanted help, rather than tell him. Peter felt he was being treated as if he were stupid. He felt demeaned and discounted by him.*

The helper person is, perhaps without realizing it, playing one-up to the other person. He or she takes pleasure in offering help, even if it isn't taken! This ability boosts the helper's ego and makes them feel important.

A number of years ago I was talking with a childhood friend who was prone to giving frequent advice. During a recent 15-minute conversation he gave me advice about three different things we were discussing, none of which I had requested. He knows it is annoying, and has three daughters and others who may give him feedback to stop doing this, as well. But it definitely has become a pattern. I don't think he realizes how demeaning it is when it is unsolicited.

I recall when I first was training to be a Gestalt therapist, and one of my teachers, Jim Simkin, Fritz Perls' co-leader in many training groups, would tease me about being a social worker who was always trying to help others.

Through working with him I saw the error of my 25-year-old ways and worked very hard to change this aspect of myself. As Fritz would often say, for a therapist to give advice or offer help is "doing the patient's work for them" and not allowing them to discover for themselves.

EXPERIMENTS

1. **Become aware of how being the helper can be 'perceived' as being one-up, and helping the one-down person, thus creating a hierarchy even if there was none.**

2. **Discuss this dynamic with your partner, both sides of it.**

3. **Experiment with being playful by reversing roles to see what it is like for each to play the other.**

4. **What it is like for you to be offered *unsolicited* advice?**

5. Yes / But

This foible can be a version of one partner telling the other what to do. In the example below, he sets her up to play the helper by telling her of a problem he has. She goes into solution-mode and offers unsolicited advice; then once he gets her advice he turns it down. This can become a regular pattern. The issue is never about the advice, but about the relationship between the one who complains and the helper who is summoned. The helper is at the top of the hierarchy. The complainer is below her. He resents her telling him what to do, so he refuses her advice. For example:

> He says: *"My leg really hurts"*
>
> She says: *"I think you should go to the doctor's right now. I'll take you."*
>
> He says: *"No, not now. I'll take care of it later."* (Yes, but: *Don't tell me what to do; don't give me unsolicited advice. Ask me.)*

EXPERIMENTS

1. **Become more aware of this pattern, discuss with your partner how it makes you both feel.**
2. **Encourage the listener not to use the word *should,* and ask him if he wants advice before offering it to him.**

> He says: *"My leg hurts and I just want to tell you about it. No advice please. Are you open to listening to me complain a bit?"*
>
> She says: *"Okay, I have a half an hour now as I have to get ready to go to town."*
>
> He says: *"Oh, great; that will be plenty of time! Thank you!"*
>
> She: *"Are you open to my giving you advice today?"*
>
> He: *"No, if you have any let's wait for another time since you have to leave soon."*

6.   'We' Versus 'I'

Some couples refer to themselves as 'we' a lot. "We love to see science fiction movies."; "We agree about everything."

These folks are often joined at the hip, as they say... experiencing themselves as one, rather than two separate individuals. (See Togetherist / Separatist chapter.)

In many cases it sounds like they have agreed to all these statements, but I'm not always sure of this. Sometimes one speaks for the other and the other, who disagrees, often keeps their mouth shut.

Years ago I led a relationship workshop in Phoenix for a Gestalt institute there. One of the trainees brought their next door neighbors, a couple, so that I could work with them in front of the student class. The couple and I were seated in a semi-circle in front of about 20 students and as we began, the husband stood up and moved forward so that he couldn't see his wife or me, as he addressed the students. He wanted the students to know what a wonderful relationship he and his wife had. So he said things like, "We have worked out our anger with each other over many years. We love each other and we feel that we are a good example of a successful relationship."

As he was saying all of these things, unbeknown to him, his wife had tears streaming down her face. During the session following his diatribe, it came out how unhappy she was in the relationship, and even though she couldn't verbalize her feelings very well, he was not speaking for her.

It was a powerful example of what can happen when one person speaks for the other, especially without their agreement. Not only was he using the royal *we*, but he was telling us how she felt, and he left her out of the process.

EXPERIMENTS

1. **Speak for yourself!**

2. **Or ask your partner if what you just said is true for her as well!**

"We," he told the group, "have a perfect relationship!"

7.   Manipulation

"We are spoiled and we don't want to go through the hell gates of suffering: we stay immature; we go on manipulating the world rather than suffer the pains of growing up."

– Fritz Perls, 1969

This is a huge topic, and one most of us are familiar with. My definition of individual manipulation is trying to get what we want from someone indirectly, without being up front and clear, to avoid being told **no**.

As little children we learn the best ways to do this in our families, since we didn't have the power to get what we wanted by ourselves. So we learned ingenious ways to do so! Perhaps you remember your ways of getting what you wanted as a young child.

The problem is that many of us continue these behaviors into adulthood and end up becoming devious and cunning in our relationships, as these ways are the only ones we know. And getting what we think we want becomes more important than the relationship between two human beings, so manipulating often leads to unhappy relationships.

I don't recall this, but my mother told me I used to be a head banger. She caught on right away to my manipulative ways and did something that stopped me. I was a toddler and don't remember a thing about this.

EXPERIMENTS

1. **Get in touch with the manipulative ways you used as a child.**

2. **Ask yourself if you still use these same ways as an adult.**

3. **Try on new more direct and clear ways of behaving.**

4. **See if you can tolerate saying NO, and hearing NO.**

5. **Discuss with your partner.**

8.   Speaking Dysfunctions

"The single biggest problem in communication is the illusion that it has taken place."

– George Bernard Shaw

TALKING TOO SLOWLY, TOO QUIETLY, TOO LOUDLY, BEING REPETITIOUS, NOT PAUSING FOR OTHERS TO DIALOGUE WITH YOU

These speaking styles can interfere with a healthy back and forth dialogue between you and your partner. The person who speaks so fast is difficult to hear and understand fully. The slow talker can lose his audience easily as their minds may wander. The quiet one demands you move closer, rather than their taking responsibility to be heard. The repetitious one thinks that you'll understand if she repeats herself a few times. The one who leaves no pauses in his verbalizing, keeps you out of the dialogue, and on a limb waiting for him to stop or pause. All of these behaviors make understanding difficult and will probably discourage others from wanting to talk to you at some point.

All of these styles may be out of awareness to those who practice them, and many of them are the results of learned behaviors in families of origin. A fast talker might have grown up in a large family and in order to be heard, felt she had to speak fast. The slow talker may have had to be very careful of how she spoke for fear of a reprimand from a parent or ridicule from a sibling. The quiet one may have been ridiculed as well for taking an unpopular stand, so he says things that are barely audible.

SILENCES

Many folks never allow a quiet moment in a conversation, but fill in the empty spaces as soon as they can. When asked, they say they are afraid of the silence. Some are reminded of how hard it was to get a word in edgewise in their families of origin, others feared the unexpected could happen in the silence, so they attempted to *control* the situation by continually talking so nothing bad would happen. This is a common pattern in my experience, and one that is often annoying to the listener, as usually the filler words have no meaning. This dynamic does *not allow* for people to reflect on what the other has said. It does not allow the conversation to find its own rhythm, as the anxious talker controls the conversation by not allowing it to happen spontaneously. (See chapter on Silence.)

When there is no give and take—whereby each listens to the other and responds accordingly—there is little chance for a creative exchange between the two of you, where your responses are the result of truly hearing each other and considering each other's point of view.

EXPERIMENTS

1. *Experiment doing the opposite of what you usually do. If you tend to talk fast, talk half as fast. See what you experience. Does your partner run away? Stay and listen longer?*

2. *If you talk slowly, experiment speeding up. How is this for your partner? or role play your partner's speech pattern with loving kindness (!) to increase awareness.*

3. *If you tend to talk loudly, try the opposite. See what you experience.*

4. *If you don't leave space for the listener to respond, experiment with stopping on occasion and asking him or her for feedback about what you are saying. See what you experience.*

5. *Experiment with allowing silence in your conversations. See what you become aware of.*

6. *Create a silent time for a specific amount of time, perhaps while on a driving trip. See what wants to emerge as time goes by.*

9.   The Hit and Run Dynamic

This one is a form of *discounting*. And it is probably quite obvious. It has two parts 1) someone says something disparaging with one or a few words or a gesture, and 2) then leaves the scene, allowing no time for a response or dialogue. He just hits and runs.

I'm sure many of you have experienced this or done this to others without awareness. Bullies do this a lot. For example:

He says: "That was stupid!" And then he storms out of the room.

His partner says nothing, as no one is there. She is in shock, and left 'holding the bag' of negative energy just thrown at him.

The Republican presidential candidate Donald Trump is a master at this. Every day during the USA primary election he threw a label at another candidate, and the audiences were left with the poisonous effects of his behavior.

This is very destructive tactic since there is no opportunity for the person being labeled to respond in person. There is no 'I–Thou' or dialogic opportunity. There is no opportunity to have an open and heartfelt disagreement or conversation about the comment the hitter is making. Unfortunately this is very common in intimate relationships. And it bodes poorly for them for the following reasons and more.

- The receiver of the Hit often experiences *rage* at both the comment and the fact that the deliverer of it has left the scene, and is unavailable to deal with his remark.
- Many feel *hurt or devastated* by both the comment and the disappearance of the deliverer.
- Others experience being *misunderstood* and feel a variety of emotions around this from rage, anger, frustration, tension, anxiety, and depression.

EXPERIMENTS

1. *Having knowledge about this dynamic increases your awareness. Then, hopefully, the two partners will engage in a sensitive and careful working through together about what happened in a contactful manner. This then, usually results in appreciation and understanding. Seeing a therapist might be required if things get too disruptive or volatile between the two.*

2. *For your own growth and understanding, see if you can differentiate between a label, such as "you jerk!"—which is a derogatory word summing up some observed behavior— and a specific comment about the person's behavior. For example: "I saw you laugh at your dog and she put her tail between her legs and slunk out of the room." The latter is a phenomenological account of what the observer saw, rather than a label. Most people prefer the latter feedback to the label.*

10. Discounting: Verbal and Non-Verbal

PERCEPTION

O ur perception of being discounted or dismissed is probably the most common cause of upset between couples and partners that I've noticed over the many years I have been a practicing therapist. When couples come into my office, what they most frequently present is that one has been slighted by the other, causing great upset in the relationship.

Please note that I said *perception*. Everything is in the eyes of the recipient, or beholder, of the event.

> *Ginger perceived that her husband was insulting her. After much work, she realized he did not mean to do this. This does not mean he did, nor does it mean he meant to. This was her perception.*

So many of our experiences are what we perceived happened.

There is an old movie from the 1950s or '60s called *Rashomon*, made in Japan. It is three vignettes in one. There are the same three people in each of the three vignettes. It is the story of a murder, as told from the point of view of each of the three persons. Each of the three vignettes is totally different than the other two. It is quite an amazing movie, and one to be seen for those interested in how multiple people can experience the same phenomenon so differently.

There is nothing static or true about perception! It exists in the eye of the beholder only!

DISCOUNTING

Discounting is experienced by most of us as shutting us down, dismissing us, ignoring us. Many of these are done verbally, and many non-verbally… and often both are involved. When a person says they feel discounted or dismissed, they are telling you their *interpretation or perception* of their experience. They are not actually telling you a feeling, even though that is what they are saying. What they feel once they say they experience being discounted can range from rage and tears to humiliation and shame. This is not to diminish our dismissive behaviors—which often stop a conversation, or point out how one member of the dialogue has no recourse. The dismissive one has summarily executed the other, often by a label, a gesture or a comment to make his contribution seem irrelevant, ridiculous, or whatever the discounter intends.

NON-VERBAL DISCOUNTING

This can be rolling your eyes, shrugging your shoulders, a hand gesture where some-one's hand is pushing the air near you away, laughing, looking away, a particular facial expression by partner. We all know these gestures. It has been said in family therapy classes that all you need to do is watch a sitcom on TV with the sound off, and you can tell pretty much what is transpiring by watching the non-verbal dismissive dynamics, as well as all of the others.

VERBAL DISCOUNTING:

There are many examples of these. For years I've asked my clients which labels do they try to avoid having others put on them. Here are some of them: silly, stupid, irresponsible, liar, goody two shoes, mommy's boy, sissy, phoney. Many of us carry these into adulthood, without being aware of it, and do everything in our power to *limit who we are,* so as not to give others reason to label us in these ways.

As a result many limit their aliveness, creativity and ability to connect with others out of fear of being labeled our most "feared" labels.

A couple are having an exchange about what do together on a Sunday afternoon. She wants to go to a movie that is up for an academy award; he wants to watch a football game on TV. Neither wants to budge off of their position, so then the discounting begins.

He: "We can't afford it. All you do is want to spend money on things we can't afford. You are flaky and irresponsible."

She: "Oh shut up! You're no prize yourself, just a damn couch potato who isn't open to anything new and adventuresome anymore. You are no fun anymore."

Often the verbal and non-verbal behaviors go hand in hand. For example, she sweeps her hand at him as she explains, "Oh, shut up." He shuts up, but later rebels and goes after her in his favorite fighting modality.

TEASING, SARCASM, MAKING FUN OF

"That was a joke. I was just teasing." Well, these are also forms of discounting. Again, it is throwing a label at the other, which is disparaging, and the person doing this is not open to a discussion or dialogue—only in putting someone down. It is a cheap shot. It is like Hit and Run. (See previous chapter.) It is as if energy from the discounter is thrown at and falls onto the other. It is not given to the other in an open way so that he or she can genuinely respond in an egalitarian give and take.

Unfortunately I hear a lot of people tease their pets. If you watch closely, the pets often respond in ways that indicate they feel ashamed. A dog will put his tail between his legs and slink off, for example. I've seen a cat turn away from the person teasing her, as if they know they've misbehaved. Contact is thwarted.

There is a game I've seen between three people, where two gang up by teasing the third. It looks harmless at first, as if the three are having fun, but notice how the one being teased is taking it. This is a form of bullying from my perspective.

> *I recall the following example when I was in 7th grade. A classmate and I were in the back seat of the car while our mothers were in the front seat. My mother explains to her friend what we were laughing about in the back seat, "That is just 7th grade humor."*

Many years later I still recall this incident. I felt labeled and discounted by my mother. There was no way out of the box she put me in. I was angry and hurt. And, of course, I didn't have the awareness or verbal skills to deal with her about that in those years.

EXPERIMENTS

1. *For starters, become aware of your discounting behavior, both verbal and non-verbal, and your partner's as well. Notice the labels you each dish out.*

2. *Notice the effect of these on the other person.*

3. *Then experiment with not discounting your partner for a week. See what you experience, and notice how your partner seems without the discounts.*

4. *Share your awareness of your discounting behaviors with your partner.*

5. *Apologize if it fits.*

6. *Ask your partner if she is open to feedback about her discounting behavior. And indicate that you are open to such feedback.*

11. Talking *At* Rather Than *To* The Other Person

Phone rings. Julie: "Hello?"

Andrea: "Hi, Julie. I just got back from the marriage counselor and she gave me a hard time about my partner. I don't know what to do about her. She said I was too lenient with him, and didn't stand up to him enough. He just looked at me, kind of smiling, as if he agreed with her! I was really upset.

(She goes on in this vein for 20 minutes, while Julie half listens as she does the dishes and answers a few emails, which Andrea doesn't seem to notice.)

Julie, who finally breaks in, says: "Andrea I'm late to pick up my dog at the vet's before they close. I need to go. I wish you luck with all of this."

How many of you have experienced something like this? Or perhaps you've been the talker? In the above example Andrea has no sense of the other. She is talking AT her rather than TO her. It is as if Julie isn't a full human being at the other end of the line. Andrea has no interest, it seems, in whether Julie has time to talk at this moment, as she doesn't ask her how she is, and furthermore she doesn't warn her of what she is about to do, talk for some time! There is no real dialogue, no back and forth discussion.

Years ago when Fritz Perls, founder of Gestalt Therapy would hear someone TALKING AT someone else, he would roll up a piece of paper to make it look like a megaphone and encourage the person to continue talking through the megaphone AT the other (with awareness). Usually the person got it with this approach! So in order to honor each person's time and space, here are some possibilities.

Talking AT, not TO you!

EXPERIMENTS

1. *Tell the speaker you only have a minute or two, if you can get a word in edgewise.*

2. *Ask them to check with you first before launching into a story.*

3. *Ask her to give you a Lead Line, (See Chapter on Lead Lines), before she launches into her experience.*

4. *And particularly if she is your partner, explain how uncomfortable you are when she didn't leave any openings for you to say something, or ask you if you have time to talk now, or would it be better to talk later, if at all!*

5. *And she didn't ask you for her feedback or thoughts about what she was saying.*

6. *This dynamic could surely warrant a few couples sessions, as it is a very destructive dynamic.*

12. Admitting Mistakes

Healthy people can often admit mistakes or indiscretions they have made, even though it often is not easy for them. This is, of course, because they know they are more than their mistakes, and they are secure enough inside themselves to weather these storms, even if it means the other can't trust or feel comfortable with him as before. The relationship can suffer, as it would if we didn't acknowledge our mistakes, so we don't win by being defensive, silent and in denial.

> *Geri: "You promised you'd go with me to the event last night, and then you said no at the last minute. I'm upset."*

> *Roberta: "You are right, I did promise. And I didn't tell you the truth that I wanted to watch the debates, so I said I was feeling sick. I have got to do better with this. I am very sorry. I understand your being upset with me."*

> *Geri: "And you even lied to me, something I didn't know until now. I'm more upset now. I can't trust you to be open and honest with me."*

> *Roberta: "I am feeling embarrassed and ashamed. I will deal with this one way or the other. I'm very sorry how much I upset you and your trust in me. And I understand this may have consequences down the line for us."*

The irony of this exchange, is Geri started out being upset at Roberta for not sticking with her commitment, and then discovers Roberta lied to her as well. If Roberta had told the truth in the beginning, she would have avoided lying, which only compounded the problem.

EXPERIMENTS
1. *Ask yourself if your truth has gotten in the way of your connection with one another. If it has, you might want to tell the truth to your partner, risking his reaction.*
2. *Build up your disappointing-others muscles.*

13. Truth Telling

Telling ourselves our truth is considered a sign of being healthy and aware. Many of us were not brought up to be truthful as we were afraid of the reactions of others, and of our own internal critic or Topdog. So it was best to keep our truth to ourselves, or deny it!

We then discovered ways to manipulate our lives and those in it! What a crazy mess this approach turned out to be. People began going to therapy to "get straight" as they used to say. We became very good at hiding the truth from ourselves. Whole schools of counseling were developed to deal with this emerging issue in so many peoples' lives.

Lying is a serious issue for many. And of course it is all tied up with how we want others to see us, and how we see ourselves. We learned to try to control perception: our own of ourselves, and yours of us. It doesn't work too well!

BAD NEWS ABOUT TRUTH TELLING

There are times when telling the truth can be done as a self-serving game. I recall years ago this notion came up in family therapy training. One client told his partner he was having an affair, and felt self righteous for being honest!

This chapter is not about being a good or bad person. It is about being self aware, and sensitive to others as well. From a Gestalt therapy perspective, we encourage our clients to tell themselves their truth in the moment. Whether they tell their partner or others is up to them.

The Paradoxical Theory of Change invites us to acknowledge our truth in the moment, which makes us congruent. In other words we are not fighting ourselves to be different than who were are *in the moment*. Acknowledging is a form of *acceptance* of ourselves. This is a strength, as in the next moment who knows what our truth will be. This congruence and acceptance allows us to be aligned, and to move on to whatever emerges in the next moment.

"In this moment I'm feeling hurt by you."

"In this moment I'm angry as you remind me of what my brother said to me as a child."

"At this moment I'm remembering how I scared him one day."

"At this moment I'm laughing as I realize we were mean to one another one moment, kind the next, playful the next."

"And at this moment I'm not feeling hurt by you anymore."

Truth telling was a value among the Navajos, where I worked for a number of years. There, many were involved in the Native American Church (NAC), which holds peyote ceremonies for the purpose of getting in touch with their truths. Although I never took peyote with any of them, I saw the results of a culture that valued self acceptance, self knowledge, truth telling and self awareness.

Here is a poem written by Mr. Tom Torlino on the Navajo Nation around 1890.

I am humbled before the earth

I am humbled before the sky

I am humbled before the dawn

I am humbled before the evening twilight

I am humbled before the blue sky

I am humbled before the darkness

I am humbled before the sun

I am humbled before that standing within me

Which speaks with me

Some of these things are always looking at me

I am never out of sight

Therefore I must tell the truth

That is why I always tell the truth

I hold my word tight to my Breast

It is so interesting that at this time in the USA, during the most bizarre election season ever, where two of the most popular candidates, Bernie Sanders and Donald Trump, are being cheered on by millions as they are perceived as telling the truth. They are both pointing out over and over again who is lying, who is deceiving us, and how that is unacceptable now. And the Establishment candidates and their followers are trying to stop them both from winning. Probably you readers know who won by now. At this time of writing it isn't clear what will happen!

What is going on in this evolving egalitarian world is much bigger than the elections in the USA and in our personal relationships. It is really part of a *paradigm shift* on many levels throughout the world. Although people have been crying out for freedom and equality for many years, it seems to be happening on a larger scale. This in part may be due to social media.

EXPERIMENTS

1. **Start some sentences, whenever you wish, with "At this moment the truth is…"**

2. **And then try on the phrase about something you don't like about yourself, "And I accept this about myself right now even if I don't like this about myself."**

3. **Try this over and over again and see what you experience, and see if you can accept more and more of who you are at any given moment, even if you don't like aspects of yourself.**

4. **Remember you can always seek help for this enlightening exercise, particularly from a Gestalt therapist in your area.**

14. Lead Lines

Have you ever answered the phone when someone was at the door or you had to go to the bathroom, or some other urgent thing was necessary at the moment, and the person on the other end of the line launched into a long story? This talkative person does this frequently when he or she is in the same room with others as well. Usually what happens is that the listener, if she isn't comfortable giving the talker feedback, will eventually find a way to get out of the situation, leaving the talker feeling somewhat discounted, and perhaps confused as to what happened. He may feel his story needs more details, so he may say it all again, embellishing the first rendition. And then he may try again, making his story even longer! And again. And again.

On occasion I've suggested talkers give the listener a *lead line* and ask them if they have a few minutes, or perhaps an hour! This allows the listener to be a part of the decision about what is happening to him! For example:

> *Jerry calls Ana and says: "Do you have a few moments? I want to talk over an idea with you."*

> *Ana may respond with: "I have dinner in the oven, can I call you back later?"*

This may feel good to both of them.

If he just launches into his idea she might pretend there is nothing pressing going on so as not to interrupt him, listen half heartedly as she multitasks, and then later wonder why she is feeling stressed out. She may avoid Jerry's calls in the future without being aware of why, and he may be confused as to why they don't talk as often as they used to.

I'm sure you get the picture and probably have experienced doing this, or having it done to you! It is a common dynamic.

Often the talker was not listened to fully to when young, so tends to be verbose with everyone, expecting they, like his parents, won't listen to him fully unless he entertains them with his stories, or overwhelms them with his words, or says the same thing in a number of different ways to ensure they understand him. Of course, none of these approaches work, for long at any rate.

Another thing to consider is that these conversations are not really conversations; they are *monologues*. There is little or no time for the listener to respond. Most people prefer a dialogue, where there is a healthy back and forth in their conversations. So a listener might be easily turned off if he can't participate in the dialogue without causing a problem.

EXPERIMENTS

1. **Discuss the ideas of Lead Lines with your talkative partner, if this is the case.**

2. **If you are the talkative one, ask your partner if your talking so much is a problem for him or her.**

3. **Discuss the idea that sometimes Interrupting is useful and that you want to try it out!**

4. **Many times people are used to being interrupted and didn't realize their partner never did that, as she felt it was rude.**

5. **Remember the importance of being present with each other, and having a dialogue, not a monologue!**

6. **Keep exploring as you increase your awareness together.**

15. Giving-In To Avoid Conflict

Unfortunately, once an egalitarian structure is put in place by a couple, the areas of disparity begin to show up. Usually these are the people who are newly in love and don't want to argue about anything. So one or both begin to abdicate and give in to their partner, even if means doing something they have strong feelings about. A pattern may begin to develop where one complies with the other to avoid disagreement. This pattern can persist for years.

The person who gets his or her way: they love it at first, but often after awhile they begin to resent their partner for not having any back bone. I've often heard: "I don't know what he wants. He agrees with me all the time. I don't really know who he is. I've lost respect for him since he hides himself so much from me." "I wish he'd stand up to me, especially if he doesn't like what I am suggesting or requesting."

The person who complies or gives in: At first this attitude may seem admirable, but if this pattern persists, this person will begin to put up protective walls around himself, begin to lose a lot of his aliveness and be less contactful. Or he may begin to act-out and attack his partner passive aggressively, by being sarcastic, making fun of him, having a secret affair, and so on.

Years ago a well known psychologist referred his wife to me for therapy. She arrived and told me straight out that since she felt her husband was having an affair with his secretary, he thought she was paranoid and needed therapy. After exploring this theme for a few weeks, the husband of the secretary called my client to report that his wife and her husband were indeed having an affair. She had chosen to give in to her husband's ideas of who she was, rather than confront him with her own beliefs and understandings. And she was grateful she was seeing me and could count on my support as she dealt with the aftermath of knowing she wasn't paranoid after all, and that he had been lying to her.

EXPERIMENT

1. *Experiment with being more direct.*

2. *Discuss the pattern you see emerging between the two of you.*

3. *Seek help to undo giving in from a couples' therapist.*

4. *Read or reread the chapter on Conflict.*

16. Just

Over the years I've come to realize the person using the word *JUST* thinks that what he is suggesting is easy to do. For him it might be, but for his partner it might be the hardest thing in the world to do!

I am forever hearing one member of a couple say:

*"If you would **just** say no."*

*"If you would **just** set limits with her."*

*"If you would **just** tell him how you feel."*

For example for some to "just say no" is very difficult. For some it is difficult to set limits, and for others it is difficult to tell their partner how they feel.

For someone who finds the above suggestions easy to do, reverse these and ask yourself to "just keep your mouth shut," rather than say no, set limits, or share how you feel. For this person keeping quiet might be the hardest thing to do.

So be aware of when you use the word JUST with yourself or your partner. And also with your children.

EXPERIMENT

1. **Try some sentences to your partner starting with "If you would just …" and fill in the blank.**

2. **Ask your partner if it is difficult or easy to do the above.**

3. **Become more aware of when you use the word JUST.**

17.   You Need to Change, So I Will Feel Better

"Men marry women with the hope they will never change.
Women marry men with the hope they will change.
Invariably they are both disappointed."

– Albert Einstein

For years women have dragged in their reluctant men to my office for couples therapy. I'd say approximately 8 out of 10 men felt they were there for their women, not for themselves. "I will be happy to go see a therapist with you, dear, to support you, as I don't need any help; you do." This was the common response of the men in the lives of a number of women. Over and over again. In those days many women felt taken care of by this response.

This response by many men has baffled me. Why is it that so many men feel so secure in themselves? Was this the way millions of mothers and fathers raised them?

This is what my colleagues and I used to discuss on a number of occasions. And we came up with some thoughts that perhaps American mothers were partly responsible for raising their sons to not need help, and to support their wives and girl friends if they needed help. It is part of the expectation that men are to take care of their wives and families, as in the old days. Also, Americans are seen as having a John Wayne mentality: you must do everything yourself and never ask for help.

Then, over the years, another interesting phenomenon began happening. Men came in to see me with the notion that their wives needed to change so that they themselves would feel better. Now this is quite a statement! Of course, they'd feel better if their women would follow their suggestions and change accordingly. However, their women rarely bought this analysis!

So back to the drawing boards again. Why do so many men want their women to change in ways to make them feel better. Why Not?

If I can put the blame on my partner to change, that would be wonderful! Especially if the psychotherapy community agrees with me!

Years ago when I was a young new therapist, a woman came to see me, feeling somewhat desperate. She and her husband had two young children under the age of 5. The mother was feeling feelings she'd never felt before, and they scared her. She reported that her children were constantly messing up the house and she couldn't control them. For the first time in her life, she began to feel anger and even rage. She wanted me to fix the children, so she would feel better.

I told her I couldn't do that, and why. I told her I could work with her on how to work more effectively with her children, but there was no guarantee that she would feel better with my help. She and I worked together for about a year, I think, and during that time she became more accepting of the behaviors of young children, lowered her expectations that they would and could keep her house clean at such young ages! They should be grown up by now, so I hope they don't have any memories of their mother's perfectionism!

EXPERIMENTS

1. *Ask yourself: "Do I like myself in this relationship?"*

2. *Ask your partner if he likes himself in your relationship.*

3. *Explore whatever comes up between the two of you .*

4. *Scan your history and see if you or any of your partners ever got trapped in this dynamic.*

5. *Did you ever use this dynamic with any of your partners, friends or family members?*

6. *Acknowledge your truth to yourself.*

7. *Acknowledge your truth to others, if it feels important to do in this growing era of transparency.*

18. We *Should* Talk This Over Now!

It is human nature to do as one is told. So in my couples classes, people often leave with all this information, a set of new tools and skills to communicate with, and so on. Rather than encouraging their partner to also take the classes, many take these ideas as "shoulds" and proceed to trounce on their partner about not doing everything "right"!

Not only that, if they have adopted the idea of having a meeting with their partner every so often to go over issues and concerns, this too may end up as a big should.

Or if a couple gets into a struggle, one might say:"*We should talk this over right now.*"

Slow down! Who says you should discuss this right now?! Again, this can be a *joint* decision as to when you talk this over. And how can you decide when to discuss differences and still maintain a loving and caring relationship.

One of you might need time alone to think about what happened. (See Togetherist/Separatist Dynamic and the Contact Withdrawal Dynamic chapters.) The other one may feel a need to smooth everything over before going to sleep. Honoring differences like these often creates a more supportive and caring atmosphere in which to discuss differences.

MYERS-BRIGGS TYPOLOGIES

For those of you familiar with the Myers-Briggs Typologies may find this idea helpful in accepting differences between the two of you.

For those of you who don't know this Jungian-based program, I encourage you to do an internet search for it and learn about it. It might help you and your partner understand one another even better.

There are 16 personality types, and what is amazing about this, is that almost every characteristic of human behavior, emotions, experiences are acceptable. So it is about diversity of all these things, and helping others to realize everyone fits into one of these types. No one is better than another. It honors differentness.

Business people use this typology to help place people in jobs most congruent with their type. Couples can learn a lot about accepting their partners by reading about this typology. You might like to read about it on-line, and take one of the tests, to see what your typology is, and your partner's.

It covers introvert versus extrovert types, intuitive versus sensing types, thinking versus feeling types, and planners versus spontaneous types.

I have used this typology with agency staffs, to help them accept one another and their differences. Couples can benefit from this as well.

Although many of us wish our partners didn't have certain qualities, whatever you come up with when taking the test doesn't mean you can't change. Extroverted people can become more introverted, thinkers can learn how to feel more, so that people can be closer to the middle line between these polarities after doing some personal work in therapy or through self exploration.

EXPERIMENTS

1. *Check out the Myers-Briggs Typologies to understand your partner and yourself now more fully. If you take the test again in a few years you may find you've both changed somewhat.*

2. *Regarding the title of this chapter, find out if your partner needs time alone to process what happened between the two of you before meeting to discuss what happened.*

3. *If you feel you need to meet as soon as possible, see if you can compromise or negotiate a time that would be acceptable to both.*

19. Silences

"Some changes look negative on the surface, but you will soon realize that space is being created in your life for something new to emerge."

– Eckart Tolle

Many folks never allow a quiet moment in a conversation; they fill in the empty spaces as soon as they can. When asked, some say they are afraid of the silence. Some are reminded of how hard it was to get a word in edgewise in their families of origin; others feared the unexpected could happen in the silence, so they attempted to control the situation by continually talking so nothing bad would happen. Difficulty experiencing silence is a common pattern, and one that is often annoying to the listener, as usually the filler words have no meaning. This dynamic of filling silences with words does *not allow* people to reflect on what the other has said. It does *not allow* the conversation to find its own rhythm, as the anxious talker *controls* the conversation by not allowing the other to speak.

Years ago when I worked on the Navajo Nation, the following story made the rounds: An Anglo and a Navajo man, who knew each other, met on the street in town one afternoon. The Anglo man said "How are you?" to which the Navajo man said nothing. The Anglo, fearful of upsetting him to ask for an answer, went on his way, waving to the Navajo and saying it was good to see him.

A week later they ran into one another again. The Navajo was the first to speak and said: "About that question you asked me last week. I've been thinking a lot about it…" (He then proceeded to tell the Anglo man how he was!)

Although this story has elements of diverse cultural styles, such as taking the Anglo's greeting literally, the Navajo man was quite comfortable with silence. For him it was natural *to take the time to reflect*. In many cultures like in the USA white Anglo world this is not usually the case, and the speed with which people talk, with no pauses to breathe or reflect, can keep things at a superficial level, with no time for the experience of the other to be stated much less absorbed.

Dialogue is avoided, so contact between two people is minimized. And often the speaker ends up talking AT (no dialogue) rather than TO (open to dialogue) the listener.

The back and forth in a conversation, verbally and nonverbally alike, allows for meaningful contact between the parties involved, like between you and your partner. As the saying goes, humans are social animals who need interaction and contact with others. We need a response and we want to give a response. It is one of the key elements of being human.

If a couple can allow silence with comfort, they may get into very creative conversations, or new ideas may come up that are interesting to both parties.

EXPERIMENTS

1. *Become aware of the amount of silence that you and your partner experience with one another. Is it comfortable? Uncomfortable? Would you like more silence? Less silence?*

2. *Discuss this with your partner if silence is an issue in your relationship.*

3. *Take a drive in silence and see what emerges between you both.*

20. I Can't Trust You Anymore

This is another common complaint I hear a lot from one party of a couple, "I don't trust you anymore." Trust me to what? Cook our dinner? Go to work? Kiss me goodnight? What is the accuser complaining about specifically? Usually it is a general accusation.

- Trust comes in millions of actions, behaviors, thoughts, and feelings.
- I don't trust you to be honest
- I don't trust you to be careful with our finances
- I don't trust you to never have an affair
- I don't trust you to get a job

There are so many specific issues the word trust can be applied to. So first of all the person who says, "I don't trust you," needs to be much more specific. For example:

John says to Olympia: "I don't trust you."

Olympia: "Don't trust me about what or to do what? Please be specific."

John: "To text me when you leave from work so I will know when you will be home, more or less."

Olympia: "I can do that, but remember I am new at texting, and I often forget."

John: "I realize that WE didn't make an agreement about this when we created the structure for our egalitarian relationship, so can we do that now?"

Olympia: "Yes, and that will help me remember, I'm sure. But don't accuse me in general like that without knowing specifically what is going on with me. You make me sound like a criminal."

So obviously to accuse someone of not being trustworthy is a dead end, and leaves the accused not knowing anything specific. And often one is criticizing her partner for something that is not so huge as to gain the title of untrustworthy!

In fact, many couples go to great lengths to be "trustworthy" and often forget their own wants and needs. Remind yourself that you are not in this world to live up to anyone else's expectations.

Since this is such a common accusation, I encourage all of us to carefully look at whether we have agreements around trustworthiness, and are they specific. This is a very deep and touchy subject for many people.

EXPERIMENTS

1. *If you tend to think in terms of trust and trustworthy, be aware of how devastating these terms can be to your partner.*

2. *Imagine your partner says this about you.*

3. *See if you can be more specific and clear with your partner and get away from generalizations, especially with this word.*

21. Expectations and Assumptions versus Hopes and Desires

"Assumptions are the termites of relationships."

– Henry Winkler

The quote above indicates a real travesty if we are prone to making assumptions. I'm sure all you readers including me have made assumptions in the past, and have been met with anger or hurt from our partners and others for doing so.

The main reason for creating a lot of this book is to make explicit what may be vague and unclear between two people living together. Being *explicit* allows each party to know a little better what to expect of the other. For example if my partner and I agree that a separate vacation once a year would be a good thing, I would then expect my partner to feel all right when I announce that I want to go hiking with my women friends for a week in the Sierras. He should expect me to suggest such a trip at some point since we discussed the idea and he agreed. And likewise, I expect him to want to plan a week somewhere without me. This is explicit and clear. No assumptions are being made.

ASSUMPTIONS

What are assumptions? They are basically guesses about another person based on something we think we know about them. For example, your partner may be seen eating some salami at a party on their first date. So his friend buys a lot of snacks with Italian meats when she has him over for dinner, and is surprised when he tells her he is basically a Vegetarian.

She had spent a long time wondering how they would get along since she was also a Vegetarian. She created in her mind, a lot of expectations, which didn't make her very happy. Needless to say she was pleased to hear he was a Vegetarian. It would have been a lot easier for her to ask him if he had any foods he couldn't eat before buying all the Italian meats for him. We are so used to second guessing people rather than asking them directly.

Someone years ago said the word ASSUME makes an ASS of U and ME.

EXPECTATIONS

Expectations are usually based on agreements made or unaware assumptions that have not been checked out with our partners. These unaware assumptions can lead to horrendous misunderstandings, hurts, anger and disappointment. So you can see how important it is to become aware of our assumptions. And to become aware of whether our expectations are based on clear agreements. Often they are not.

For years Jerry assumed everyone agreed that it is not good to interrupt others. He was sorely wrong with this assumption! In many cultures and families it is the modus operandi. So his anger at being interrupted made his life miserable until he got it that he could not expect this from others automatically. He eventually learned to ask for what he wanted and his partner luckily agreed to not interrupt.

HOPES AND DESIRES

If I hope for something, I don't expect it. I just hope for it. I desire it. Therefore if it doesn't happen I might feel disappointed, but not necessarily angry since there was no agreement, thus no expectation.

So being explicit about who you are with your partner, allows this person to see and hear you clearly. The two of you can make agreements so that you each know what you can expect and not expect from one another, thus lessening the possibility that he or she will misunderstand you and make assumptions about you!

What you are explicit about today may not be true for you tomorrow.

So remember it is okay to change your mind. Yes, men, it is okay for you, too! What you hoped for last year might not be true at this moment in time.

EXPERIMENTS

1. *Discuss with your partner those things you hope will happen in your relationship together about all kinds of things, to make explicit what is implicit.*

2. *Discuss your hopes and desires and how these are different than your expectations.*

Section H

Conclusion

Summary

Acknowledgements

Covenant of Community

Bibliography

Summary

In this book I've covered a little of the history of psychotherapy in the USA since the Human Potential Movement of the 1960s with Fritz Perls and Virginia Satir, who were major contributors to this movement. Fritz brought the existential approach of Gestalt therapy and Virginia brought her approach to family and couples therapy to the Human Potential Movement. Both of these teachers, who shared their approaches with one another at Esalen Institute in California, emphasized that they did not follow the medical model, as traditional psychotherapy did at that time, but rather called their approach part of the emerging growth model. The medical model saw its customers as patients who had illnesses; the growth model saw its customers as fellow human beings who were not sick, but on a path of self-discovery and awareness.

GOOD WILL

One of the key items between two people who love and care about one another is *goodwill*. Goodwill can carry people through good and bad times, painful and upsetting times. Do you feel this towards your partner and from her as well? Even when you are in the throws of resentments and hurts?

I reviewed how Gestalt therapy was and still is dedicated to people being equal. Virginia Satir's family and couple's therapy orientation, is also based on the notion that people are equal. In a world of so much conflict and hierarchical organizations, governments and structures, it is hard to see our equality much less honor it daily. Some of my colleagues and I have noticed that most of our clients come into therapy because of *relationship issues*, revolving around issues of equality, respect, and caring.

MOST PEOPLE HAVE NOT MUCH EGALITARIAN EXPERIENCE

Over the years while teaching Gestalt therapy, it occurred to me that most Americans have not had much experience in egalitarian organizations or relationships during their lifetime. And so many do not know how to operate within one, working together with others for the good of the family or unit. And many nowadays have not had a Civics class in school where they've learned about democracy. This is a very unfortunate byproduct of our society.

Children are under the thumb of parents, schoolteachers, and then employers, and when old enough and skilled enough they probably then become the parents, teachers and employers. But where are we equals? Most say only in friendships, and these don't include living together or working together... so this doesn't add up to much experience.

It is no wonder that many come to therapy to work on their relationships, which by in large are seen as egalitarian since the 1970s Women's Movement in the USA, even though most don't use this term.

CREATING EGALITARIAN RELATIONSHIP STRUCTURES

For the last year and a half I've led classes where participants experiment with each other in developing a structure for an egalitarian relationship—one where both parties decide together what the nuts and bolts are of their day to day lives: who does the cooking, whose monies are used for what, who takes care of the pets, the cars, the bills, the outside of the home, the inside of the home, and the psychological concerns. Participants had numerous eye opening experiences about issues they'd never thought to consider as part of an egalitarian relationship such as asking your partner if a friend or relative can come visit for a week. Some people believe that if they are relatives they are welcome into their home whenever they please. And not every partner makes this same assumption.

In some of the classes people changed gender during the role playing to see what it might be like to be the opposite sex, and people learned a lot from doing this that they had never thought of. One man was amazed that his desire to take a road trip by himself, as role-playing a female, was okay with his spouse. Some still behaved as if they were men and women from their grandparents' generation where women did the cooking, cleaning, and men earned the money.

Assumptions upon assumptions were discovered in the classes, much to everyone's surprise. A lot of discussion followed to reconsider a number of practices each experienced in his own relationship that needed clarification and understanding if they wanted to have a more explicit egalitarian relationship.

They all got that it didn't matter what they decided as long as they both agreed. So one could be the main breadwinner and the other could stay at home, watch sitcoms and eat chocolates all day, as they depicted middle class women did in the 50s with the advent of washing machines and dishwashers which made the work of housewives much less, or so they thought. Joint decisions were key, over and over again.

Vague agreements and lack of clarity caused problems. And over time these joint decisions needed revisiting as couples aged or got different jobs, or moved to a new community.

More psychological issues were addressed. The importance of setting aside a regular time and place for couples to discuss how they are doing as a couple and sharing their feelings and disagreements with one another. Do they know how to deal with differences, conflict, hurt and anger.

CALLING YOUR RELATIONSHIP EGALITARIAN

This book is dedicated to those who want to define their relationships as egalitarian, and want to be explicit about who is responsible for what. They want to emphasize the importance of honoring their equality in all ways. And they want to be part of a growing egalitarian movement in the world.

HEALTHY RELATIONSHIPS

I explored aspects of healthy relationships. One ideal type of relationship is where people can come together, connect, and then part to do other things in their lives, and come together again, in a healthy rhythm where both are independent human beings who are dedicated to being with one another as long as they are able to pursue their own interests and desires, including work and play. Not everyone can do this all of the time, particularly if illness and other unforeseen things happen to one or both parties, which means one may be more dependent on the other for awhile.

This still can mean they are equal.

These ideals are not to be taken as *shoulds* but as guidelines to be experimented with, to try on to see if the new approach fits. This is very important. If it doesn't fit, don't do it, as it could be counter-productive for you both. You hopefully can find other alternatives that you can both agree to. If you can't find other ways to work for you both, and you find yourself hurt, angry, resentful, or behaving in dysfunctional ways, causing even more problems. At such times, when people feel stuck and at an impasse, help from someone trained in family or couples therapy could be of enormous help. And if you can find someone with a strong Gestalt orientation, that would be an even greater plus.

IMPORTANT THEMES

Here I explored some important themes that are relevant to most relationships:

- Each person's personal rhythm of Contact and Withdrawal
- The Separatist and Togetherist Dynamic, and how it affects intimacy between two people
- The high and difficult expectations of the Success and Failure Model where everything is judged according to one or both person's concept of success and failure. There are other models of living!

UNHEALTHY DYNAMICS

And lastly I explain a number of common unhealthy dynamics between two people, not only couples but others as well. These 21 short chapters give you a brief sense of each one. And if you are like most of us, you may have a few of your own to add to this list.

If one of you tends to give-in to the other to avoid conflict, see this as a red flag, as it can come back to bite you in the future. Each needs to be able to say what they think, what they would like, and what they feel to their partners, so that they can negotiate and hopefully come up with win-win solutions.

EXPERIMENTS

At the end of most of the chapters are some exercises you can experiment with to increase your awareness, your choices, and your egalitarian experiences. As a Gestalt therapist I prefer learning by experience, as we tend to integrate such learnings more readily or regurgitate them more quickly if they don't taste right to us.

And here is one more experiment for you before you finish this book: These are guided fantasies for you to explore your world and your relationship more deeply.

GUIDED WORLD FANTASY

- Imagine you are a bird, an ET from outer space, an Angel or God and you are looking down at the Earth. Notice all of the hierarchical relationships from this vantage point in countries all over the world.
- Zoom in on different countries and notice if there are any egalitarian organizations or governments. Do you see any?
- Imagine more of these are created everywhere you go. What do you see? How do the people like these co-operative organizations?
- Or do people prefer to be told what to do and not have to worry about working together with people they might disagree with?
- Discuss your experience with others.

GUIDED PERSONAL FANTASY

- Imagine you are with your partner or create one if you are currently single.
- Imagine you are discussing your relationship with this person. If you don't have an egalitarian relationship, imagine discussing one, and what that means to you.
- Discuss specific things you want in your relationship that you don't have now.
- Listen to your partner's response *fully*, allowing him or her to have their full say.

CONNECT WITH OUR DEEP INNER SELVES AND OUR PARTNER'S

More and more people want to connect with each other on a deeper and a more authentic level during these chaotic and changing times. A new paradigm is forming that calls for more of us to step forward in authentic ways. A more egalitarian way of life is emerging in all aspects of life as more and more people learn to work through some of their dysfunctional roles and games.

These changes will be an enormous boost to our world as we learn to *see and hear* our loved ones more fully and to honor them with good will, compassion, caring, respect, support, and at times, tough love, all of which requires spending more quiet time with one another, away from our favorite distractions, as we get to know each other better.

These are also similar messages to some "growth model" counseling orientations like Gestalt therapy, and to those from some important religious and spiritual teachers of our times.

Your ideas and feedback are always welcome! You can reach me through my website.

Cyndy Sheldon, MSW
Bellingham Washington, USA

www.CyndySheldon.com

July 2016

Acknowledgements

There are so many colleagues and friends and clients to thank, I do not know where to begin!

After spending a few years learning about Gestalt Therapy from founder Fritz Perls, MD, and James Simkin, PhD, I realized something was missing—working with relationships and couples. Virginia Satir was becoming well known at that time, and I sought training through her orientation and became a staff member at the Family Therapy Institute of Marin in San Rafael in 1968, where I worked for six years under the direction of Marti Kirschenbaum, PhD, and Shirley Luthman, MSW, the directors. I received excellent training from them and was fortunate to continue on teaching through other venues afterwards, with Kay Hall, MSW, Rusty Dillon, MSW, and Joe Busey, PhD. Old friends and colleagues Erich S, Diana L, Alyssa H, Betsy H and Brian H, Bettina P, and my ex-husband Carl Werthman, who has passed away, were valuable contributors to my learnings and teachings over the years.

From this point on, many students over the years, and many couples who came to me for therapy taught me what was important to them. And to all of you I send my thanks. My own personal experiences in long-term relationships and a marriage, of course taught me a lot! And most interesting was the therapy my ex-husband and I got when we couldn't decide whether to divorce or stay married.

Now, many years later, I am sharing these ideas with Gestalt trainees in the Seattle-Bellingham area of Washington State, and with many who have taken my recent classes on how to create egalitarian relationships. Thank you to Patrick D., Rebecca T., Lindsey W., Adam W., Ryan T., Ruth H., Betsy W., Amanda B., Alexis G., Emma W., Lia A., Francis A., Ambur T., Lea E., and others who attended my classes, experimented with new ways of being with a partner, and gave me feedback about their experiences, much of what has informed this book.

And lest I forget, the sketches on the front and back cover were done by Angela Anderson, and those inside by Paula Forget. How grateful I am for your whimsical drawings.

I thank you all!

Covenant of Community

Association for the Advancement of Gestalt Therapy
www.aagt.org

Because Gestalt therapists encourage, respect and support alternative voices, value non-confluent relationships by owning and expressing differences, engage with resistances as "the energy, not the enemy," identify and work with polarities in the field, and honor dialogical processes as the heart and soul of Gestalt methodology, the "Covenant of Community" was developed and approved at AAGT's 2002 Gestalt Conference, with a recent addition of item "I" at the 2013 Annual General Meeting following a months-long AAGT members' Internet dialogue on social equality and justice. This was done to provide supplemental guidance for and a commitment to creating and sustaining dialogue in our Gestalt community. The "Covenant of Community" invites AAGT members to subscribe to the following dialogical processes, particularly when encountering dramatic differences:

A. We will undertake and encourage one another to engage in ongoing dialogue with one another and to remain open and in contact when choosing to withdraw temporarily from dialogue.

B. We will undertake to recognize, acknowledge and own our projections, to check out our assumptions, and to encourage one another to do so.

C. We will undertake to maintain community through patience and understanding.

D. We will undertake to support the needs of the members of our community.

E. We will undertake to stay with even difficult dialogue, acknowledging the need for space and refreshment when hungry, tired and frustrated, but not abandoning one another.

F. We will undertake to get and remain interested in the impact our behavior, words and intentions have on one another.

G. We will undertake to put our desire for and interest in power (in whatever form) out on the table along with being honest and direct in other arenas.

H. We will undertake to attend carefully to language or other communication that objectifies the other.

I. Moreover, we will undertake in whatever way emerges through our experience with the larger social field to support the purpose and ethical values of our community, which include the human worth and dignity of every person. In this way we declare our commitment to social equality and justice among persons within our community and in the wider, external community.

Bibliography

Angry White Men, Michael Kimmel, Nation Books, 2013.

Bright-Sided, How The Relentless Promotion Of Positive Thinking Has Undermined America, Barbara Ehrenreich, Holt Books, NY, 2009.

Covenant Of Community, aagt.org

Do I Have To Give Up Me To Be Loved By You, Jordan and Margaret Paul, Second Edition, Hazelton Publ., 2002.

Diagnostic and Statistical Manual of Medical Disorders, Vol. IV & V, American Psychiatric Association, 2015.

Everybody's Life is Worth a Novel, Erving Polster, PhD, Gestalt Journal Press, 1987.

Gestalt Awareness, edited by Jack Downing, MD. *Chapter: Women and Gestalt Awareness*, Lois Brien, PhD, and Cynthia Sheldon, MSW, pp 91-103, Harper and Row Inc., 1976.

Gestalt As A Way Of Life, Cyndy Sheldon, MSW, 2013.

Getting Clear, Anne Kent Rush, 1969, Pub: Random House and Bookworks.

The Handbook of Body Psychotherapy and Somatic Psychology, edited by Gush Marlock, Halko Weiss, Courtenay Young, Michael Soth, North Atlantic Books Publ. 2015.

I and Thou, Martin Buber, new translation by Walker Kaufmann, PhD, Touchstone edition by Simon and Shuster, 1971.

Intimate Enemy: How to Fight Fair in Love and Marriage, Richard Bach, 1983.

Intimate Terrorism, Michael Vincent Miller, PhD, Norton Pub. 1995.

Legacy From Fritz, Patricia Baumgartner, PhD, Science and Behavior Books, 1975.

Patriotic Betrayal, Karen Paget, Yale University Press, 2015.

Psychotherapy For Women: Treatment Toward Equality, Edited by Edna Rawlings, PhD, and Dianne K. Carter, PhD. *Chapter 6: Gestalt Therapy for Women,* Lois Brien, PhD, and Cynthia Sheldon, MSW, pp 120-128.

Satir Step By Step: A guide to Creating Change in Families; Conjoint Family Therapy; People Making, all by Virginia Satir and Michele Baldwin, Science and Behavior Books, Palo Alto, 1983.

Your Body Works: A Guide to Health, Energy and Balance, edited by Gerald Kogan, PhD, Transformations Press, Berkeley, CA. 1980.

You're In Charge: A Guide to Becoming Your Own Therapist, Janette Rainwater, PhD, DeVorss & Company, 1989.

You might also be interested in Cyndy's first book

GESTALT AS A WAY OF LIFE

Out of the body of existential teachings of Gestalt Therapy, emerged a number of practices we were invited to do as students of the Gestalt founders back in the 1960s. What are you aware of right now; give your headache a voice and have it talk to you; slow down and breathe; be more present when we connect; stop qualifying; be more specific; lose your mind & come to your senses; say that louder; tell me your truth in this moment.

This book delineates a number of these principles and practices, offering some experiments for you to do. If you are able to do most of these without getting stuck you are in danger of becoming more aware, more alive, more contactful, more creative, and maybe more enlightened as well!

"This book speaks with an enchantingly simple voice, enhancing our understanding of the everyday concerns of living. It offers the kind of modest human spirit with which most people can identify; yet it goes disarmingly deep as it transforms a revealing look into life-as-it-is into the promise of life as-it-could-be."
– Erv Polster, Ph D, Gestalt Therapist Emeritus, author of many books including *Gestalt Therapy Integrated,* and *Everyone's Life is Worth a Novel.*

Cyndy Sheldon, MSW
Books available at
www.CyndySheldon.com
or Amazon.com

Made in the USA
San Bernardino, CA
30 June 2016